I WAS HITLER'S MAID

I WAS
HITLER'S MAID

BY

PAULINE KOHLER

First published 1940 John Long Ltd
Republished 1993 Christine Stockwell

ISBN 0 9516640 3 4

Printed and Bound in Great Britain by
Woolnough Bookbinding,
Irthlingborough, Northants

To

BOBBI SCH.

INTRODUCTION

THIS IS A BOOK OF FACTS ABOUT HITLER, facts which, until now, have been unknown to the world. I was a servant at Berchtesgaden. I had a unique opportunity of seeing the real Hitler. I saw him when he no longer had the eyes of admiring crowds upon him. It has been said that no man is a hero to his valet. It is even truer that no man is a hero to his maid.

I escaped from Germany. As I write this in the free sunshine of France I know that in a few days I shall be sailing for Brazil to build up a new life there. But I want the world to know the real Hitler, to know the truth about his private life, about his women friends, about the men who surround him, about the secrets of the mysterious mountain chalet of Berchtesgaden.

Everything I reveal I have myself seen or have learned from unimpeachable informants. I have tried to present a true objective picture. In parts the picture is an unpleasant one. But then the truth about a man like Hitler must always have its unsavoury side. And if this book helps those who are fighting against Hitlerism to understand something of the supreme enemy of civilization I shall feel that the years of horror I spent at Berchtesgaden have not been entirely wasted.

I WAS HITLER'S MAID

CHAPTER ONE

I WAS IRONING SHIRTS AT MUELLER'S LAUNDRY in Karlsruhe when Adolf Hitler entered the Reichstag as Chancellor of Greater Germany for the first time. I was happier than he. I was in love.

Ten days later I was married. Kurt was foreman of Mueller's packing department. Two days after that, while Kurt and I were honeymooning in Berlin, I got a telegram from my mother telling me that my father had been arrested. He was a Social Democrat and an ardent trade union worker. When I returned to Karlsruhe I found that my parents' flat was empty. Frau Scholtz, a neighbour, told me that the Gestapo had taken my mother too.

I have never heard of either of them since.

I was heart-broken. But worse was to come. Mueller's assistant foreman in the packing department was jealous of Kurt because my husband was a much younger man. He wanted Kurt's job. So, like hundreds of others all over Germany, who took advantage of the Gestapo's zeal in hunting down the enemies of the Reich, he denounced my husband to the police. Four S.A. men came to our flat at midnight that night. They dragged Kurt from bed beside me and kicked him down the stairs to a car. It was the last time I saw him in Germany. Within three weeks of marriage I had lost my parents and my husband.

I have deliberately avoided emotion in recording these facts because the only three people in the world I cared for have no real place in this story except to explain why in an agony of despair and loneliness I became a domestic servant. I left Karlsruhe when I had not a penny left in the world, to become maid-of-all-work to a schoolmaster and his wife at Munich. I obtained the post through a friend who was living in the citadel of Nazidom.

My experience in the first few weeks of Hitler's power had taught me one important thing. Never under any circumstances to discuss politics. I told Frau Hornbach, my new mistress, nothing of what had happened. She did not know I was married until one day she found me crying in the kitchen.

She seemed kind from the beginning, and, desperate for a little sympathy, I told her everything. She was very sympathetic. She released in me all the pent-up emotion that I had concealed and fought back for many weeks. I committed an irretrievable error. I cursed Adolf Hitler.

As soon as I had calmed down Frau Hornbach sent me to bed. She was very sympathetic indeed. She made me feel much better. She was also a good German citizen. She told her husband. He was on the telephone within two minutes and, again at midnight, two jack-booted S.A. men arrived at the house.

I knew it was hopeless to protest or to struggle, so I dressed quietly and went down to the slick new limousine the S.A. men had commandeered for the use of the Party, which was the way the Nazis obtained everything they wanted at that time. Few people cared to protest against this theft of their property, though they were forced to sign documents saying that they had voluntarily lent it to the Party.

My guards were not more than twenty years old. I am—or was—not an unattractive girl. (I was twenty-three.) The youths sat on either side of me in the back of the car. They began to exchange obscenities about my figure. I tried not to listen. Said one of them mockingly : "Do you think they're real, Lutze ? Or is it one of those bloody French tricks ?"

The other one replied : "Well, it's easy to find out. What's holding you back ?"

I bit his hand.

Lutze struck me in the face with his fist. A huge gold ring on his finger cut me over the eye.

I submitted to the man-handling for the rest of the journey. When we reached police headquarters I was taken before a young captain by the two S.A. men.

"What's the charge?" he asked.

"Slander of the Führer and intrigue with enemies of the Reich already under arrest."

"Take her to Koch."

I was hustled down a corridor to a small room filled with tobacco haze where a paunchy, middle-aged man sat back in a swivel-chair with his feet on the desk. His face was mottled with red splotches, and his teeth, when he opened his mouth to roar at my guards, were sepia-coloured and broken. I shuddered.

"What's she here for, black or white?" he growled at the S.A. men.

"White," said Lutze's companion.

I discovered later that this meant I was merely under suspicion and not the object of any specific charge or the victim of any particular Nazi's personal venom. It was, in fact, rather lucky for me. 'Whites' may and are very often released early from the concentration camps.

Sergeant Koch began to take an interest in me.

"You'll be out in no time, little girl," he said. And then added with a leer, "if you're a good girl and do as you're told."

I shivered again. He saw it and scowled.

"You'll learn not to be so sensitive here, you little bitch."

He picked up the telephone, pressed a button, and said: "Send Anna up to me."

Anna, brown-smocked and so bulky that even Koch seemed slim beside her, came up two minutes later. Her face was as hard as ferro-concrete as she gazed at me, while Koch filled in a form. He handed it to her and said: "Sign for the new pigeon, Anna."

Then he winked and said, "Look after her carefully as a favour to me. She's rather sensitive."

Anna did not even answer him, but she seized my arm and jerked her thumb towards the door. I went meekly.

The women's section of the Munich police prison was fuller than ever in its history at this time. Ninety per cent of the hundred and fifty who were sisters in distress with me had been rounded up within the past month, and most of them were married. Their crimes were that their husbands had incurred the hatred of the Nazis. Some of them were calm enough, but most of the younger ones were constantly on the verge of hysteria.

Before I was allotted to a cell, however, I was taken for medical examination. This, I discovered, was an excuse for the young Nazi doctor in charge to compel any young or attractive girl to undress before him and run lewd hands over her. The older women he used to pass as O.K. without even a second glance.

Next I was given a bath. Two burly wardresses scrubbed me with floor-brushes until I was scarlet. Then they pushed me under an icy shower.

One of my cell-mates was a middle-aged housewife of the good, solid middle-class type. Her name was Mittelmann, and she seemed more overcome by the disgrace of going to prison than by the thought of its discomforts at the hands of the Nazis. She wept continually and moaned, "What in God's name can I ever tell my family of this thing?"

Her eyes were puffed and red with crying, and wisps of faded grey hair kept falling over her pathetic face. She was a quite pitiable object.

The other inmate of Cell 79 was more interesting. She was a Jewess. She told me her name was Jetty, but I never found out her surname, for she was taken away from Munich to Dachau next morning.

Jetty had the most hauntingly beautiful eyes I have ever seen. They were great blue-black orbs that fascinated you and impelled your undivided attention when they gazed at you. They gave her pale oval face an unearthly nobility. She was the wife of a doctor who had already fallen a victim to the terror. Brownshirts had shot him in the back when he was trying to escape from his home after a friend had telephoned him to warn him that they were on the way.

The shock of his death had made Jetty indifferent to her own fate. She was always reproaching herself with his end.

"Oh, Pauline," she choked, "he would have got away in time if I had not held him in my arms so long. I couldn't bear to let him go. I loved him too much. I killed him, Pauline, I killed him."

I soothed her and told her of my own husband's arrest. I was terrified that something had happened to him and that I should never know. And, in helping me to find comfort, Jetty forgot her own troubles.

Then she told me of the treatment at the prison where she had been for three weeks. She warned me never to show my feelings at the sights I would see, and to submit to the obscene behaviour of the S.A. men when I was called for examination. "You are much more likely not to be bothered if they see that they can't upset you than if you are obviously horrified," she said.

Most of the Nazi officials at the prison were cases of sex complexes, it seemed. Probably the wretched creatures were affected by the atmosphere in which they spent their days and nights. Sadism, of course, was the commonest complex. The cruelties inflicted were beyond belief. The first time I saw a girl stripped and flogged till she fell in a bloody heap in the exercise ground I fainted from sheer horror, but I became hardened to worse sights than that in the coming weeks.

But it was the little unpleasantnesses that affected me mostly on my first day in prison. There was no sanitary accommodation, for instance. Jetty, Frau Mittelmann and I had to share a dirty bucket.

We had no uniforms and were allowed to keep only the dresses we were arrested in. Apparently, a change of clothes was considered too great a luxury for political prisoners.

My first meal, too, made me sick. It consisted of a tin

mug full of an evil-smelling stew in which lumps of black soggy bread floated wearily. There was also a piece of dry bread and a mug of water. I refused to eat it at first, but Jetty said : "You ought to eat it, my dear. They will simply take it away if you don't, and the Nazis won't care very much if you starve to death."

I forced myself to eat. I vomited. Half an hour later I tried again. I managed to hold it down this time.

No lights were allowed in the cells and we rolled ourselves in the single blanket allowed each prisoner and tried to sleep on our straw mattresses at half-past eight when dusk came. It was then September.

At five a.m. a wardress opened the cell door and told Jetty to get dressed.

She obeyed calmly and before she went she kissed me and said : "I don't expect I shall see you again, Pauline. Good-bye, and be brave. Remember, *this* hell is not eternal. The one these creatures face goes on for ever."

The wardress struck her across the face and dragged her out into the corridor.

I wept until we were told to get up at six o'clock.

Breakfast was a piece of liver sausage and a chunk of dry bread, washed down with watery, tepid coffee.

Frau Mittelmann told me some more of her immediate history. Her husband was manager of a department at the Munich gas-works. He had worked there for twenty-five years. He had never taken any interest in politics, but one day, before Hitler seized power, he had told his assistant, a zealous Party man, not to bother his head with politics and not to get mixed up with hooligans who fought at street corners like the Nazis did. The assistant remembered those words and, like my own husband's assistant, he denounced his superior to the Nazis and got his job as a reward.

"But you, Frau Mittelmann," I said. "Surely they have nothing against you ?"

"I was so upset that I told my neighbour I thought Hitler was a blackguard," sobbed my cell-mate, "and she told the Gestapo."

It seemed incredible that respectable citizens should be flung into jail on such flimsy pretexts, but it was only too true in Munich at that time.

My first three days in prison passed fairly uneventfully. It was a routine of rising, washing, eating, parading in the exercise yard and returning to our cells. We were not allowed to work since, theoretically, we had not been sentenced to prison, but merely awaited trial on the fantastic charges that had been brought against us.

Occasionally, at night, I heard screams that made me shiver, but no one ever spoke about them.

On the fourth day we were all ordered to the exercise yard at eight a.m., two hours earlier than usual, and I wondered what was to come.

We were drawn up in two ranks and as we stood to attention under the eye of Anna, the gross head wardress, four Brownshirts appeared at the entrance gates. They were dragging behind them a curious wooden contraption.

At first I thought it was a gallows and my heart sank. But I noticed two arm-holes in the side pillars, which were, anyway, too short for a gallows, and curiosity replaced my fears. Not for long.

It was a flogging-block.

The four Brownshirts stood two at either side of the block in silence, staring at us for about three minutes. Then the Governor of the prison, accompanied by the young doctor who had examined me, entered the yard. Behind him, held up by two wardresses, came a young woman prisoner I had not seen before. I discovered later that she was a new arrival who had been so outraged by the 'medical examination' of the doctor that she had picked up an inkstand on his desk and cut open his head with it. I noticed this morning that he was wearing a big piece of sticking-plaster across the left temple.

The Governor addressed us.

"Prisoners," he said, "you are going to witness an example of the punishment meted out to those who attempt violence against the upholders of law and order."

The Governor stood aside. The half-fainting girl was

B

handed to the Brownshirts. Two held her by the arms while the doctor tore off her blouse, broke the straps which held up her underslip, and let the garments fall to the girl's waist, leaving her torso naked. He then placed a stethoscope against her heart (which could scarcely have been beating) and signed to the two Brownshirts to fasten her to the ghastly wooden instrument of torture.

They fastened her ankles to the base of the side-pillars with small chains and thrust her unprotesting arms through the holes provided for the purpose.

For the first time she now seemed to become aware of what was happening to her. A heartrending groan escaped her lips. She looked at us, drawn up in deathly-still silence, with a wild appeal in her eyes. It was agonizing. Every woman in the yard, except Anna, who was used to such scenes, must have felt as tormented as the victim.

The fourth Brownshirt took up a position behind the prisoner and slashed the air with a many-tailed whip. The lashes whistled. A shudder ran down my spine.

Then the Governor lifted a hand. The first blow fell. The sounds of the tails striking the soft young flesh brought involuntary screams from half a dozen women among us. The victim's cries were drowned by them.

We saw half a dozen dull red weals across the girl's back. Eleven more strokes were delivered with all the force of the flagellant's muscular forearms. After the sixth, the girl's piercing shrieks stopped. She seemed to lose consciousness. The flogging went on.

After the twelfth stroke the Governor ordered the man to stop, and again motioned to the doctor, who gripped the poor creature they had half-killed by the shoulders, jerked back the drooping head, and looked apparently into her eyes. He made no attempt to examine her back, which was crimson with gouting blood.

He turned away with a nod to the two wardresses who stood by while the men unshackled the prisoner. Before the woman could grab her, she collapsed in a bloody quivering heap on the asphalt.

One of the men suddenly appeared with a bucket of water, which he emptied over the girl. It revived her and she began to groan. The man hoisted her to an upright position and the two wardresses held her under the arms and began to drag her away. . . . The Governor addressed us again.

"The penalty for attack on prison officials is death. This girl has been spared. Let her just punishment be an example to you, and, remember, if you try to emulate her, you may not be as lucky in retaining your life. Dismiss."

Lucky !

Anna gave us the signal to march back indoors, and we were quickly shepherded to our cells to prevent the spread of hostility and indignation becoming serious. They knew that when we had cooled down there would be few who would dare to make any practical protest.

I have seen twenty-three women flogged in German prisons, but because this was the first experience, I suppose, it affected me most deeply. I was almost unconscious as I walked into my cell, and when Frau Hornbach began to weep and wail about how awful it was, I simply fell into a dead faint on the floor. The good woman revived me with the only few drops of water we had in the cell. She told me I had been 'out' for nearly five minutes. Two days after this, Anna came to my cell in the afternoon and said in her toneless voice : "Come with me."

I knew it was useless to ask Anna why, so I followed her with my heart working overtime. What had I done ? Was I to be flogged ? Might I, merciful God, be released even.

I was taken to the young captain who had briefly interviewed me on the first day I arrived. His name was Muegel.

He stared at me for about a minute before he spoke, looking me slowly up and down with eyes that did not conceal their owner's thoughts. . . .

When he did speak it was to order Anna from the room.

"Wait outside," he said. And Anna waddled out without a word, as usual.

Then Muegel opened a thin file of papers on his desk and read them closely.

The Nazis, with their customary efficiency, knew everything about me. I was amazed at the details they had patiently dug up from heaven knew where.

At last the captain addressed me. He said : "Did your father teach you to believe in trade unionism and Social Democracy ?"

I replied with perfect truth that I had never had any interest whatever in politics and that I had even refused to join a trade union at Mueller's laundry.

This seemed to please the young man. But then he said : "What about your husband ?"

"Kurt was not interested in politics either," I told him.

"But he and your parents are under arrest, you know. What about that ?"

I declared heatedly that they had all been arrested on false evidence by people who had grudges against them.

Then I asked eagerly : "Please can you tell me where my husband is and my father and mother ?"

The captain smiled and shook his head. "I'm afraid I don't know where they are," he said.

He pondered over the file of papers for a few moments and then said : "There doesn't seem to be much evidence against you—except of course on the charge of defamation of the Führer. That is a very serious charge."

I tried to explain that I had not meant what I had said and that I had been overwrought when I did say it, and that I had never before or since even mentioned Hitler's name.

Muegel got up from his desk and walked round to me. "I think you might get out pretty soon," he said with a smile.

My heart leapt with joy and I almost burst into tears as I said : "Oh, thank you so much, sir, thank you."

But Muegel had not finished.

"That is if you behave yourself here. But I'm sure you will. You know I rather like you. And I have a little influence in this place."

He came closer and I noticed that he was breathing rather heavily. His face seemed suddenly heated. He had a curiously strained expression.

"In fact you're a beautiful girl, Pauline."

I was terrified. I wanted to scream. Then I remembered what Jetty had told me about submitting to the attentions of the Nazis instead of struggling uselessly to stop them. I tried to feel calm. I even forced a smile. One tiny drop of cold perspiration fell from my forehead on my nose. Muegel was pressing himself against me now. He suddenly gathered me in his arms and began to kiss me.

I thought of Kurt. I thought of my happiness a few weeks ago. It seemed like ten years.

A hand, trembling slightly, stroked my breast. It felt moist through the thin silk of my cheap little blouse. The man's whole body seemed to vibrate with passion.

Slowly, he released himself from my arms and led me towards a settee. I began to cry. He sat down and pulled me to him. He began to unbutton my blouse. . . . I was still weeping when Anna was summoned to return and take me away. She remained as impassive as ever, though it was perfectly obvious what had happened. Her only comment to me was: "Button yourself up. We won't have sloppiness here." I stumbled to the door in a daze. I took a last look at the captain. He was smoking a cigarette and reading at his desk. On the settee lay his belt and revolver holster.

.   .   .   .   .

I suffered mental torture for nearly a week afterwards at the thought of what had happened to me and at the expectation of what might come. But I had still the hope that Muegel would keep his word and help me to go free.

It was not to be. My next move was to Dachau. Dachau—the name that German mothers use to frighten naughty children. The news was given to me by Sergeant Koch. He showed his dreadful teeth in a grin of amusement when he saw my reaction to the news.

"You'll learn to be a good Nazi, dear," he laughed. "They train erring little girls in the right kind of politics at Dachau. And, another thing you ought to be glad about is the handsome men you'll meet. I'm sure they'll take to you."

I made no answer.

By the way, I should say that I was found guilty (in my absence !) of the charge of defaming Hitler and sentenced to six months in the women's section of the Dachau concentration camp.

I said good-bye to Frau Hornbach, who was overcome with horror at my fate (though I suspect it was really terror that her own might be the same) and to one or two other women I had become friendly with at the prison. Then, with five other women, two middle-aged and three quite young. One of the older women was a Jewess and so was one of the girls. We were all in a state of panic. We were taken to the station in a police-van in which we were placed in small cells facing each other. Two S.A. men rode in front and two stood on the rear step.

They used foul words to us through the grille in the rear door. But none of us cared. We were getting hardened.

We reached Dachau at seven o'clock one November morning. It was bitterly cold and the camp looked terrifyingly grim as we stepped from the van that had collected us from the train. We went through the familiar routine of registration, medical examination and bath—with two exceptions. One, the doctor. He was an elderly man and a kind one. When I was taken before him and automatically began to undress he stopped me with a smile. "I don't think you need take your clothes off just yet."

He must have sensed what was in my mind for he then added : "You know, all doctors are not alike."

He asked a few questions about my health, made a superficial examination and then dismissed me—still fully dressed.

The other exception : our clothes were taken from us and we were given a pair of coarse artificial wool combinations and a smock of what appeared to be sacking. We were allowed to keep our own stockings and shoes.

I was again allotted to a community cell. Three others were with me this time. They were old-timers. They had been there for more than six months. I shall not bother you with their names for I am not going to dwell for long on my stay at Dachau. It lasted only nine weeks. Too many books, alas, have been written about the concentration camps for me to add with a far less graphic pen the tale of human suffering that their barbed wire fences enclose.

I must, however, mention one appalling episode. I saw a woman tortured to death for the first time.

She was a Jewess. Her name was Berta Binauer. One day she was reported by a wardress for disobedience and was sent for by the camp commandant because she was a wild spirit and had a bad record for misbehaviour. She had been flogged once. On this particular day she was being marched off by two S.A. men who had been sent for her. I happened to be about ten yards behind the little party as it crossed the exercise yard. I had been sent with a message to the camp kitchens. Berta suddenly screamed, snatched a knife from the belt of one of the men and plunged it into the other's back before she could be stopped. A sentry on the other side of the yard gate was the only other witness apart from myself. I stood spellbound. The uninjured S.A. man had struck Berta to the ground but he seemed to be hesitating about leaving her to run for help for his comrade who was groaning agonizingly. The sentry opened the gate and rushed in, unslinging his bayoneted rifle. He sent the S.A. man for help and then began kicking the wretched Jewess in the face as she tried to rise. He roared curses as he lunged at her; I think the girl must have become demented because she was screaming back at him and managed to get to her feet. She even tried to grapple with him, blood streaming from her face, where the jack-boot had struck it. The man felled her with his fist and she lay writhing as he kicked her ferociously again. Three S.A. men arrived at the double with a stretcher and two of them picked up the stabbed man while the third ran to the sentry. I was standing too far away to hear what they were saying and I was too spellbound to move.

Suddenly they picked the Jewess up and dragged her to the wooden wall of one of the huts which flanked the yard. The sentry then plunged his bayonet through her stomach and pinned her writhing body to the wall. Blood spurted out in great fountains.

Then the men tore at her clothes until she was half-naked and began to kick her systematically. They broke both her legs. The sentry next grabbed handfuls of her hair and tore them from her scalp. She must have been unconscious for a good deal of the time for she uttered only a few moans after the bayonet was driven into her. Before the sadists had finished she was dead. They stood looking at her broken body for a few minutes. Then the sentry withdrew his bayonet, let the body fall and wiped the steel of blood on her clothes.

The S.A. man went off indoors and the sentry returned to his gate. I crept indoors myself.

When we were all out for exercise two hours later there was no trace of the scene. It was never mentioned by anyone again as far as I knew. In fact my cell-mates refused to believe my story because the girl had not been punished publicly.

There were, of course, many floggings at Dachau. Revolting repetitions of the scene at Munich which I described earlier, except that a steel triangle was used instead of the wooden gallows device.

But even physical suffering, when witnessed with

monotonous regularity, can cease to affect the most
sensitive soul—if it has survived the earliest shocks.

Actually, Dachau was salvation to me personally. I was
liked by the wardresses and the head wardress and I gradually became a sort of trusty with many little privileges.
Moreover, I made an actual friend of a prison official.

I am not going to reveal this person's name or even
whether the official was man or woman. That person
as far as I know is still at Dachau and if he or she were
accused and found guilty of helping me as they did,
death would be the inevitable punishment when this book
reached Nazi Germany.

My friend secured my early release, lent me eighty
marks and gave me the address of an hotel in Augsburg
where I might get a job as a kitchen- or house-maid.

And so I said good-bye to Dachau on January 26th,
1934. I was examined once more by the kindly old
doctor (no one is allowed to leave bearing marks of
punishment), told to sign a document that I had been
justly treated and that I would never discuss in the
outside world anything I had seen or heard in the prison
camp, and given back my own clothes.

As I travelled to Augsburg, I wondered whether I
should say anything of my past or whether I should
pretend to be just a domestic, looking for a job. I
decided on the bold course because I knew that a reference might be taken up with the schoolmaster at Munich
and that things might go hard if I was proved a liar.
I planned to rely on my early release from Dachau and
my good political record.

I was to be disappointed. The manager of the hotel,
Hermann Schlief, was unable to give me a job. Times
were hard in Augsburg and he had, in fact, recently cut
his staff by more than half. But seeing my obvious
disappointment and realizing my desperate financial
plight, he recommended me to go to the villa of one
Herr Kastner, who, said the manager, had been in the
hotel only a few days ago, grumbling about the shortage
of domestics in Germany.

I had had no time to tell Herr Schlief of my prison record before he had turned me down. Otherwise, I am sure, he would not have sent me to the pleasant villa on the outskirts of the town. For Hans Kastner was a high official of the Gestapo, though I was not to discover this for several days.

I was interviewed by Frau Kastner and I told her frankly that I had been to Dachau, though I emphasized my early release and declared that I had been wrongly accused in the first place. She seemed rather astounded, I recalled afterwards, and though her expression did puzzle me, I put it down to the surprise of a woman who was meeting a concentration camp ex-prisoner for the first time. She told me at length that she would make a decision by the next day. I pointed out that I had nowhere to stay and very little money. After much thought the lady said I might stay the night and work for my keep.

The Kastners were in fact very anxious to secure a maid, I later discovered, though they had one other servant, a cook, who had a heart of gold, although she was huge and terribly ugly, and not at all popular with Herr Kastner. He would have dismissed her if she had not been such a first-class cook who could not be replaced. As it was, she was never allowed to show her face outside the kitchen.

I think I made a favourable impression on the master of the house straight away. I served dinner that night. Kastner was a thin, professorial-looking man, with an almost completely bald head. He seemed kindly enough, though rather severe in his speech.

At that moment I would never have dreamed that he had ordered the death or imprisonment of scores of innocent 'enemies of the Reich.'

He sent for me to his study after dinner and questioned me in great detail about my imprisonment and the charges made against me. As he talked he made notes on a little pad. I knew later that he was going to check up on me, though, at the time, I merely thought he was acting in keeping with his pedantic character. In the event, I was engaged temporarily. This was to enable him to communicate with Dachau. I suppose my utter frankness and my innocence of the daring required thus to beard the Nazi lion in its den made a favourable impression.

There were other reasons too—as I discovered later.

Paula, the cook, revealed to me my employer's position in the Gestapo as I was cheerfully helping her to wash dishes one day, happy to be in a comfortable home again. I was astounded. So much so that I dropped a great tureen on the floor of the kitchen and saw it smash into a dozen pieces.

Paula, of course, had assumed that I knew everything, and it was only by accident that she had talked of the Gestapo. I had not, at this stage, told her of my own experiences with the Nazis.

I trembled. I was amazed that I had been engaged. For a moment, I thought it was a new trick to hold me until I should be dragged off to prison again.

Nothing more was mentioned, however, of my record by Herr Kastner. And at the end of a week's trial I was told by his wife that they were pleased with my work and that I could stay permanently.

Frau Kastner was a pleasant woman, a good deal younger than her husband and not unattractive. Her hair was still blonde and untouched by grey, though this may have been artifice for she was inclined to be vain about her appearance and dress.

The Kastner villa was used on many occasions as a sort of unofficial G.H.Q. by the local Gestapo. Kastner's lieutenants would call on him about twice a week after dinner and they were often closeted in the study until the early hours of the morning. I was warned by my mistress never to go near the study on such occasions. She herself usually went out to the theatre or to visit friends.

One night after such a 'cabinet meeting' had broken up much earlier than usual, and while Frau Kastner was still out, my master rang the bell and when I reached the study, which was thick with cigar haze, ordered me to collect the glasses from which the party had been drinking and to clear up the room. As I was putting the glasses on a tray, Herr Kastner, who had evidently been drinking more than usual, for his normally precise speech was thickened and blurred, said : "You did not know who I was when you came here, Pauline, did you ?"

I was startled by the suddenness of the question, but I tried to keep my composure and replied : "No, sir."

"Suppose I accused you of coming here deliberately to spy, and that I had found you searching my private papers ? Do you know what would happen to you ?"

I went cold but I was outwardly calm as I said : "I'm sure you would not make such an untrue charge against me, Herr Kastner." He pondered for a moment and then chuckled : "Of course I wouldn't, my dear, I like you too much. I even believe that we are making you a good Nazi. Well, clear up the things and be off."

I was glad to escape so easily and hurried back to the kitchen. I was puzzled by the incident, as well as frightened, and I confided in Paula.

She treated it lightly. Her only comment was : "All men are devils when they're drunk, dear. My husband used to black my eyes when he'd had a drop too much, God rest his soul. But he was the best man in the world when he was sober.

"Don't you worry. Herr Kastner will have forgotten he spoke to you by the morning."

I was relieved and went to bed in a happier frame of mind. I discovered the real meaning of the affair a few weeks later when I had almost forgotten about it.

Frau Kastner went away for a week-end to stay with a sister who was ill. At about ten o'clock on the Saturday night, Herr Kastner went to bed. Half an hour later, as I was reading in the kitchen and enjoying a last cup of coffee, the bell from his bedroom rang.

I hurried upstairs and knocked at the door. "Come

in," said my master. And his voice was that of a man quite sober this time.

"Bring me some coffee and a sandwich, will you, Pauline."

I said: "Yes, sir," and went back to the kitchen relieved, for I had felt an instinctive apprehension.

When I returned with the tray, placed it on the table beside the big four-poster bed and was turning to go, Herr Kastner said: "Just a minute, my dear." His voice was silky. And I knew what was coming. . . .

I was amazed, because he was an old man to me. I suppose he was about fifty-five or sixty. And he seemed anything but virile. He pulled me on to the bed. I made no attempt to refuse because I well knew the fate that would follow if I repulsed the advances.

I even made myself as pleasant as I could for about this time I had conceived a great idea. I planned to make myself popular with every important Nazi I could meet. And I hoped as a result that I might secure the freedom of my husband. In that hope I was doomed to disappointment, but my plan worked well enough in an altogether unexpected way. It took me eventually to the home of Adolf Hitler himself—to Berchtesgaden.

The satisfaction of Herr Kastner's desires became a regular occurrence after this. He would send for me to his bedroom whenever his wife was out of the way. Apart from this unpleasantness to which I became hardened, life at the villa ran smoothly for me. Until, when I had been there three years, Frau Kastner began to suspect the *liaison* between myself and her husband. I sensed rather than knew this. Her attitude became suddenly cold and hostile, though for a long time she apparently sought proof in vain.

One night I heard the Kastners having a tremendous row in their bedroom. It had obviously been over me, for next day Herr Kastner summoned me to his study. He was in a black rage.

"You will have to leave at the end of the week, Pauline. We are getting another servant."

That was all. I departed for the kitchen and asked
Paula what I should do. She advised me to approach a
domestic agency in Augsburg, and as there was a shortage
of servants I was quite hopeful of getting another job.
I was not unduly depressed. Frau Kastner scarcely spoke
to me during the last few days. I was sorry for her
really, but how could I explain that her husband revolted
me but that I preferred to suffer his attentions rather
than be denounced as a spy ?

I was summoned to Kastner's study again a few days
later in the morning. He said :

"Would you be willing to work for the Führer,
Pauline ?" I was astounded, but I thought he meant
political work of some kind and, in case it might be a trap
to test my loyalty to the régime, I answered immediately :
"Yes."

Then Kastner told me, to my utter amazement, that
there was a vacancy on Hitler's household staff. I could
not imagine why they had considered me as a candidate,
but I believe it was because I had almost no friends and
certainly no relatives with whom I was in contact in
Germany. Also, as I found later, my appearance had a
great deal to do with it. Hitler cannot bear ugly or even
plain women in his household. Even the humblest
kitchen-maid at Berchtesgaden must be pretty.

As if sensing some of my thoughts, Kastner said : "I
am going to recommend you for the post because I believe
you have had your lesson in what happens to enemies of
the Reich and I believe that you are now a good German
citizen and that you are willing to become a good Nazi
Party member. You will, of course, have to join the
Party."

I thanked Herr Kastner with my mind in a whirl. I
was half terrified and half elated. I knew, moreover,
that such a post would place me among circles who could
surely secure the release of my husband if they wished.

Next day a Nazi car called at the villa and two officers
of the Gestapo with Herr Kastner helped me to carry my
luggage from the villa. I said good-bye to Paula, who

did not know whether to be so rry or envious. Frau Kastner never even said farewell.

I was driven to the Augsburg police headquarters, and after a wait of an hour I was ushered into a big room where a thin, cold-featured man, with one of those indefinite personalities that you find difficult to recall a day after you have met them, sat at a bg black and chromium desk. That man was Heinrich Hiimmler, most dreaded citizen of the Third Reich.

He said very little to me, but concentrated on examining a dossier about me which lay on the table before me. He looked at me carefully from head to foot. He seemed to be measuring me with some standard in his mind.

The few words he addressed to me, too, seemed to be aimed at discovering how I spoke rather than to obtain any information. He seemed satisfied at length. He signed a document and rang a bell. An official was in the room in a second. To this man Himmler gave the document and an order to take me to Department J. Here I was handed over to two women who inspected my clothes, both those I was wearing and those I had in my trunks. They told me the lot must be scrapped. I was not sorry, for my wardrobe was in a pretty bad state.

Dressmakers were summoned and I was measured for a complete new outfit. This was not ready for two days and in the meantime I was not allowed to leave the police station, but I was made very comfortable, and in fact treated as a person of some importance. During the two days I was also sworn in as a member of the Nazi Party and given a badge and number.

My new outfit arrived. Every garment was of the finest black silk. On the left breast of the uniforms (of which there were three) was an embroidered Swastika. I was told that all my other belongings were to be taken away, except a few trinkets and personal possessions. I was also told to remove my wedding ring, though, of course, I was allowed to keep it. Apparently, the symbol of marriage to any man was incompatible with service to the Führer.

When the last formality had been gone through, I was taken to a car with my much reduced luggage and put into the back seat with a Gestapo man. Two others sat at the front. We set out at once for Berchtesgaden. I tried to question my companion about Hitler's home, but he told me I would find out everything soon enough for myself, though otherwise he was very polite. When we reached the Leader's mountain fastness after speeding up the narrow private road, which was patrolled by S.S. guards every few hundred yards, I found that it was not easy to reach the house even with a pass signed by Himmler himself. We waited for five minutes at the great main entrance while our credentials were checked by telephone to Augsburg. Machine-gun crews on either side of the drive had their weapons trained on us the whole time. When we were passed as O.K. we still had to wait every fifty yards while elaborate steel barricades were removed.

I was taken straight to the servants' quarters and there handed over to Otto Schlieben, the head of Hitler's household staff (Paula, the Führer's sister, who is officially housekeeper, is really not in control of the servants).

Schlieben was one of the first Storm Troopers. He also fought with Adolf Hitler in the Great War. In one battle, half his lower jaw was shot away, and in spite of the plastic surgeons whom Hitler has ordered to operate on Otto's face it is now always set in what appears to be a terrible grimace. However, he seemed at first to be a human, kind-hearted fellow.

He told me that I was to be a housemaid and that my salary would be 100 marks a week (about five pounds), an unheard-of wage for a maid. He gave me a short lecture on behaviour, told me that I would not be allowed to communicate with anyone in the outside world while I was at Berchtesgaden and that death was the inevitable penalty for indiscretion.

Then he summoned another maid, a strikingly beautiful girl, and ordered her to show me to a room that had been prepared. My room was on the topmost storey of the fortress home. It was furnished with a small bed, a wardrobe, a chair (hard) and a simple dressing-table. There was also a small table of the kind used for taking afternoon tea. It seemed out of place. On this table I saw a small booklet. It was typewritten and bore on the cover the one word: RULES.

I was never to discuss, even with my fellow-workers, what I might see in Berchtesgaden. I must not discuss politics. I must not approach any part of the building to which I had not been expressly ordered. I must write no letters, nor must I keep any diary or record of my life. I must never fail to report to Schlieben after three hours by myself, except at night. I must be in bed with lights out at nine-thirty p.m. unless my duties kept me up later. I must never whistle (this, I found, is because the Führer hates whistling). I must never go into the gardens except on duty or in the company of at least four other employees during regulation exercise hours. I must on no account address the Führer unless he spoke first to me. This was heavily underlined. And whenever I saw the Leader I was to lower my head but, strangely enough, not give the Nazi salute or say 'Heil, Hitler' when he might address me.

The girl who had shown me to my room came back in a few minutes and took me downstairs (we were not allowed to use any of the lifts). In the kitchen, a colossal room, I was given the best meal I have ever had in Germany.

Before I had much time to take in my new surroundings or to talk with my fellow-workers, it was time for bed. I spent a sleepless night after my first day in Berchtesgaden. I was half excited, half afraid. I wondered what I should do. I wondered what I should see. I wondered if I would make good. I was Adolf Hitler's servant. What would Kurt say if he knew? Would I ever be able to get him out of prison? Surely I could save him and my parents. I would ask Hitler himself. Then I remembered the warning that I must never speak to the Führer. It was dawn before I fell into a doze.

C

CHAPTER TWO

I DID NOTHING DURING MY FIRST DAY AS Hitler's maid. A Storm Trooper named Erik Keitner was deputed to show me every room in Berchtesgaden and, after this tour of inspection, I was expected to know my way about without asking further questions.

I had read in the German newspapers that Hitler lived a simple, unostentatious life. In a few minutes I realized how the simple, trusting German people were being misled. For Berchtesgaden is a miniature palace, furnished with every luxury that money can buy.

Keitner was quite cynical about it. As he showed me the main dining-room he smiled and said, "You see, of course, how the Führer appreciates comfort. Only the best is good enough for him." This particular room is sixty feet long by forty feet wide. A massive oak table runs down the centre. There are no lights visible. A soft glow comes from cunningly concealed lighting. Four etchings by Dürer hang on the walls. A vast Persian carpet covers the floor. Later on it was part of my duty, together with another girl, to lay the table. When the dinner was an informal one the service was of magnificent Dresden china, but when important guests were present they ate off solid silver—most of it plate from the Jewish merchants of Nuremberg, stolen from them by Himmler's agents. The room in which Hitler receives his guests overlooks the Austrian Alps. The largest window in Germany covers one entire wall. I never could understand why the Führer met his guests in this room because conversation is almost impossible as it houses his aviary of rare birds. One day I counted them. There are seventy-eight—all chattering and screaming at the same time. The only time I saw Hitler display any normal kindliness and humanity was towards these birds. He always fed them himself. The death of one of them brought tears to his eyes. Its little corpse was buried in a small plot of ground with a tiny headstone of bronze placed on the grave.

Berchtesgaden has fourteen bedrooms for guests, excluding those for the staff. Each bedroom has a private bathroom. Each bath is made from stone and marble quarried from different parts of Germany—with one exception. The marble of Hitler's bath comes from Italy. It was a present from Mussolini.

The walls of the bedrooms are of bare grey plaster decorated with paintings from German mythology. On the ceilings naked fauns and nymphs disport themselves in scenes from Greek legends. Every bedroom has a bookcase by the bed. A signed copy of *Mein Kampf* is there, together with pornographic French books imported from Paris. And every room has a portrait of Hitler over the bed.

The kitchens at Berchtesgaden are magnificent. All cooking is done by electricity. A former head chef at the Adlon Hotel in Berlin is in charge with four younger men under him. The chef himself cooks only for Hitler. A Gestapo man is present night and day in the kitchens to ensure that no poison is introduced into the food.

As I was being taken round on my tour of inspection Keitner estimated how much certain furnishings had cost. Many walls are covered with rare Gobelin tapestries. "Actually, they are priceless," declared Keitner, "but if they were offered for sale in America they would fetch at least £1,000,000."

"But how can the Führer afford them?" I gasped.

"Well, there are ways and means," smiled Keitner. "The Führer can, for example, request a museum to 'loan' him a tapestry, or he can suggest to a wealthy industrialist that it would be wise of him to send him a present. Some of them, too, were just stolen from one of the ex-Kaiser's many castles."

Many of the pictures were modern. It has been part of the Propaganda Ministry's policy to hold big exhibitions of 'degenerate art' in which paintings by some of the great modern masters were held up to ridicule. But after the exhibition had closed, many of these same pictures found their way to the walls of Berchtesgaden.

There are five rooms in Berchtesgaden which have never been photographed. I saw them once and once only. They are called the Chambers of the Stars. They form a kind of penthouse high on the roof. Only two people can enter them at any time—Hitler himself and his astrologer, one Karl Ossietz.

In the main room of this suite the ceiling is made of dark blue glass on which, by pressing a switch, the movements of the planets and constellations are shown. The best optical workers in Jena worked on this room for over a year before Hitler was satisfied with it. Designs of the Zodiac form the patterns on the walls. In another of these rooms the only illumination comes from a brazier which burns night and day. Hitler often spends hours alone there gazing into its angry glow, or staring into a huge crystal globe, trying to see the future in its shifting shadows.

Ossietz is a slim, dark man of thirty-five. Few people know of his existence. In Germany no mention of him is allowed to be made, yet he is perhaps the most important man in the Third Reich outside Hitler himself. How he met Hitler no one could tell me. He just arrived at Berchtesgaden one day and has remained there ever since. He is the Rasputin of Nazi Germany. I believe he is sincere in his attitude to astrology. He believes that he can foretell the future from the stars and planets and Hitler is convinced of his powers. Shortly after I arrived the Führer spent three days and nights in this suite alone with Ossietz. Goering arrived from Berlin with urgent news—but even the fat Field-Marshal could not speak to Hitler until he emerged.

For Hitler is superstitious. He consults the stars before embarking upon any major activity. He would sooner listen to the advice of Ossietz than to counsel from his General Staff. I should say that Hitler and Ossietz have together amassed the finest collection of books dealing with the occult that the world has ever known. Museums and libraries throughout Germany have been ransacked for these volumes and every Embassy has been given instructions to buy and send to Berchtesgaden every occult book published abroad.

Hitler believes his lucky colour is red. He chose the swastika as his emblem because he had read that it was an ancient Hindu sign of good fortune—but he made the mistake of placing it the wrong way round, so that to occult students it now is a symbol of evil.

Every member of Hitler's staff hates Ossietz. They are all jealous of his influence. Goering, in particular, detests the man. He refused twice to stay in the same room with him. But Ossietz remains. Perhaps it is because he has told the Führer that he will still be ruling Germany when he dies and he fixes the year of his death as 1962.

It is well known that Hitler never drinks alcohol, but it is not so well known that his favourite drink is a mysterious concoction prepared by Ossietz. No one could tell me what it was. Irreverent members of the staff called it 'Adolf's Tonic.' It is a pink liquid, produced by Ossietz from his private laboratory in thin glass flasks. Hitler drinks three of these flasks every day. And again no one knows what effect they are supposed to have.

This laboratory was one of the few rooms I never saw. I found no one who had seen it. But Ossietz spent every moment in it, apart from the hours he passed at the Führer's side.

Perhaps it was as a warning that I was given a glimpse of the precautions that are taken at Berchtesgaden to protect Hitler. Only a trusted friend of Hitler's or one of the staff could even attempt to assassinate him within the walls of Berchtesgaden.

The whole estate is ringed by three concentric circles of anti-aircraft guns. Every approach is heavily mined. Every door into the house is fitted with an 'electric eye' which, if anyone tries to enter unobserved, immediately sounds an alarm and automatically locks every door within the building. The door to Hitler's private study is fitted with a variation of this 'eye' which can detect if a visitor is carrying any steel or iron object—not that any visitor is likely to, for, with very few exceptions, every one who comes to Berchtesgaden is thoroughly searched before being allowed to meet Hitler.

Hitler always works at an enormous desk. A battery of buttons decorates one corner. One is a brilliant scarlet in colour. Hitler has only to touch it to flood every room except the study with clouds of tear-gas. And the moment this button is touched an alarm-bell sounds in a barracks which stands some five hundred yards away and a hundred picked Black Guards, armed with sub-machine guns and hand grenades, advance on the house.

From Hitler's private suite a lift drops three hundred feet through solid rock to six rooms forming a luxury flat, which is also the last word in air-raid shelters. It is fitted with its own water supply, air purifying plant, and kitchen. One room is stocked with enough canned food to last four persons for three months.

Hitler enjoys a cinema show, so he has a small private cinema seating twenty-five persons. He sees there films which the rest of Germany are not allowed to see. It has often been said that Hitler knows nothing of the atrocities perpetrated in the concentration-camps. This is untrue. He knows everything about them. Films have been made of life at Dachau and Buchenwald and they have found an appreciative audience at Berchtesgaden. They have not been carefully censored films. Indescribable tortures have been flashed on the screen for Hitler's enjoyment.

Much of Hitler's time is spent in the map room. He has a mania for maps. Each wall is lined with shallow drawers containing maps of every part of the world. Some of them are on an extremely large scale. He has survey maps of London which show individual houses. He seemed to find some satisfaction for never having travelled in poring over these maps. Over the fireplace in this room is a gigantic bronze map of Germany and

Central Europe. The frontiers of the Third Reich are traced out by a narrow line made of amber from the seashore of East Prussia. Hitler was fond of standing in front of it with a pointer in his hand, rather like a school-master, and delivering lectures on the greatness of Germany and the way her frontiers must spread and spread and spread. His interest in political geography is intense and so he has every school text-book on the subject sent to him for his personal examination. If he is not satisfied with the maps in it, he orders the whole edition to be scrapped. Whenever we guessed that some new coup was afoot we always said it was because Hitler had got bored with the map and wanted to change it.

One of the most important rooms in the house is the telephone switchboard. Three men are on duty there night and day. A direct and private line runs from Berchtesgaden to Berlin and Munich. There is no pos-sibility of anyone ever tapping it, for when Hitler speaks his words are 'scrambled'—jumbled up into a meaningless gibberish by an electrical device. At the receiving end a similar gadget translates the gibberish into good German. This line is kept open for every second of every day and is linked with a 'phone in Hitler's study and his bedroom. He has, however, given strict instructions to the half-dozen people allowed to use it that he must only be disturbed on big questions of major policy.

Next to the switchboard is the private post office. Here all incoming mail is sorted and every letter that is not from a very close friend is opened. Everyone who is allowed to write privately to Hitler has some sign that he writes on the back of the envelope. But what the sign is I never found out. I foolishly asked about it and was told to keep a severe check on my curiosity. One or two people in Berchtesgaden believed, however, that no sign protected the contents of a letter from the attention of the Gestapo agents and that Hitler was as much spied upon as the smallest Storm Trooper.

About six hundred letters a day arrive at Berchtes-gaden when the Führer is in residence. Most of them come from Germany. About fifteen per cent come from abroad—mostly containing requests for his signature, a request which is never granted. The other letters ask for money, lay complaints, ask for a job or some favour. Hitler sees none of them, but if the writer is obviously a good Nazi he gets a letter with a rubber-stamp signature of Hitler and a promise that the matter is being investigated. Then the letter is passed on to an appropriate branch of the Government. No parcel is allowed in the house. It might contain a bomb. So parcels are opened in the barracks and the little presents which the Germans have sent their Führer are confiscated by his Black Guards. The first Christmas I was there over 11,000 parcels arrived.

There are two radio sets at Berchtesgaden, both capable of receiving any station in the world. One is Hitler's private set, the other is housed in a small radio room and connected with a hidden loud speaker in every bedroom. By pressing a switch a visitor can listen to a German station—he is not allowed or expected to hear any foreign programmes. Hitler himself knows no language but German, but he occasionally listens to music from foreign stations—particularly if it is Wagner.

A high-powered transmitting set also stands in the radio room. Few people know of its existence yet it one day may be of vital importance to Germany and the world. The wavelength on which it operates is secret, but in every big Nazi barracks there is a small set in the commander's office which is kept 'alive' and tuned in to this wavelength at all hours. When he wishes, Hitler can command his men throughout Germany without a second's delay. And there is something which only about four men in Germany are supposed to know. It was revealed to me—how or by whom I cannot say. It would mean instant execution for someone still under Nazi rule if I disclosed how the information came to me. Whenever Hitler decides to make a public appearance, he makes a gramophone record. This record proclaims martial law throughout Germany, refers to a sudden attack launched upon the security of the Reich by foreign elements, and makes a frenzied appeal for loyalty to the Führer. Himmler has persuaded Hitler to make these records. Each one is slightly different, for each one must sound up-to-date—as if Hitler were speaking at the moment. This record would be played if Hitler were assassinated. It would first be transmitted to the Nazi barracks and then rushed to Munich and transmitted over the ordinary radio. Its purpose is to conceal the fact of Hitler's death from the world for as long as possible and make certain that the country is prepared to meet any internal revolt if the news did leak out. You can be sure that such a record came out of its hidden, closely guarded safe the night when the bomb exploded in the Munich beer-cellar.

I saw two more things during my preliminary tour of Berchtesgaden. They throw a significant light on the morality of Hitler's Germany.

With Keitner at my side I was going along a corridor when I paused to look out of a window.

"What on earth are those women doing there?" I asked. A group of fashionably dressed girls, some wearing fur-coats, were just strolling out of the entrance to the Black Guards' barracks. They were laughing and giggling together and turning to wave and blow kisses to the barrack windows.

Keitner guffawed.

"Don't stand there grinning!" I snapped. "Who are they?"

"Ah, I see you've a lot to learn about life at Berchtesgaden," Keitner said. "Well, I'll explain that little mystery. The Guards are not allowed to leave Berchtesgaden for a year after they arrive here. The Führer and the Gestapo think it wise to keep them from mixing with other people. And, as you know, young men in barracks often get lonely. So the Gestapo—really a much maligned institution—provides them with company, with female company. Those girls come from Munich. They arrived last night, and now they are going back to Munich. A fresh lot will be here next week-end."

It was true. The women I saw were some of the fashionable street-walkers from Munich.

"They'll all get the Iron Cross, Second Class," joked Keitner, "for services to the defenders of the Führer."

But to me it did not seem like a joke. I was shocked. I began to realize something of what Berchtesgaden was really like.

I wanted to leave at once but knew that it was impossible. But I shook Keitner's hand off my arm and began to hurry to my room. But he caught me up and swung me round to face him.

"What's the matter? Not shocked, are you?" he demanded. "Well, there's still something you haven't seen. And I wouldn't like you to feel that your tour of inspection has been incomplete."

I had to obey him and so went down into the cellars under the house. There is nothing obviously sinister about them—they are not the dark cobwebbed vaults that cellars so often are. They form a large clean suite of rooms—but they are without windows. Bare electric lamps cast a yellow glare from the roof. The first room I entered was empty except for a vaulting-horse such as you can see in any gymnasium. The second room was fitted up as a sparsely furnished office with a desk in one corner, a metal filing-cabinet by its side, and a few deal chairs standing about. The third room was different. It was really nothing more than a corridor running past four cells. The doors of the cells were of iron bars.

I must have looked horrified—and puzzled—for Keitner began to explain.

"The cells are empty just now, but we'll soon have them filled.

"They often serve as temporary homes for the girls of the household staff who misbehave. Sometimes girls from the neighbouring villages are brought here for questioning if we have any reason to suspect their racial purity or their loyalty to the Führer. We find we can examine them so much more efficiently than the local officials. After a few hours down here they talk very freely."

For a moment I thought Keitner was crazy. Surely Hitler's home was not being turned into a private concentration-camp. But a glance at his face told me he was speaking the truth. Soon I discovered for myself the use to which these cellars were put.

Five weeks after I arrived at Berchtesgaden I had to take food to the prisoners in these cells. There were three of them, all girls round about twenty. One of them was almost naked, lying cowering in the corner. Great angry blood-red weals marred the whiteness of her back. She shuddered as I spoke to her.

"No ! No !" she screamed. "Leave me alone ! Leave me alone ! I can't stand any more."

I was alone in the cell section.

"Look ! Look !" I said in an urgent whisper. "I'm a friend. Can I help you ?"

It was several minutes before she rose to her feet and then staggered to the bars of the door. Then, in a rush of whispered words, she told me her story.

She lived in Munich and had come to stay for a short holiday with friends at Muhldorf, a village a few miles from Berchtesgaden. A young Storm Trooper had made her acquaintance. Before a few days had passed he was making violent love to her. She became frightened and refused to see or speak to him. It was a mistake. She knew that now. For he was a mechanic in the garages of Berchtesgaden and on his return he told his fellow Troopers about her. They got together and decided she might have committed some offence which they had a duty to reveal to the authorities.

So one night they descended upon Muhldorf and brought her back to Berchtesgaden. When I saw her she had been there for four days—four days and nights of ghastly horror.

Her food was thin soup and black bread. A brilliant light was kept burning in her cell for every hour out of the twenty-four. Three Storm Troopers had criminally assaulted her the night of her arrival.

She told me, too, the purpose of the vaulting-horse I

had noticed on my first visit to these cellars. She had been stripped and strapped down across it and flogged with a riding-whip. A gag, brutally stuffed into her mouth, had muffled her screams and mercifully she had fainted after about the fifteenth stroke had cut into her quivering flesh.

I could do nothing for her except whisper words of comfort and promise I would try to use what little influence I had to secure her release.

I spoke about her when I returned upstairs—to Fräulein Oberstet, who had a position equivalent to that of an English housekeeper. She was a middle-aged spinster with thin lips and a sallow face. She frowned angrily when I mentioned this girl.

"She is none of your business," she snapped. "Forget her—unless, that is, you too would like to spend a few minutes on the vaulting-horse."

Next day the girl had gone. I never found out what happened to her but I can guess. A pistol shot probably ended her sufferings.

I made several visits to these cellars. One of them was to witness the 'disciplining' of one of my fellow maids. Fräulein Oberstet accused her of insolence and sent her to her room. An hour later we—the maids— were told to go down to the cellars. Fräulein Oberstet followed us. No men were present. A few moments later the erring maid came in.

The Fräulein made a speech in which she announced that rigorous discipline must and would be maintained among the female staff. She went on to say that she had called us together to see the punishment she meant to administer to any girl who was insolent or insubordinate.

She picked four of us out and ordered us to fasten the girl to the vaulting-horse. We obeyed her. There was nothing else we could do. That girl had courage. She allowed us to strap her down without screaming or struggling. Then, still following the Fräulein's orders, we partially stripped her. The Fräulein picked up a birch and began to flog the maid. She gave her twenty strokes —but the maid never made a sound. Blood, though, trickled from her lips where she had bitten them in the effort to restrain her cries.

The millions of Germans who have spent ten pfennigs on a picture postcard of Berchtesgaden have not the faintest ideas of the horrors that are enacted behind its white and brown walls—horrors only exceeded by those within the barbed wire of the concentration-camps.

Berchtesgaden is Hitler's real home. But he has another retreat which few visitors see. I only entered it once. It is within view of Berchtesgaden—a building of steel and glass on the summit of 6,000-feet-high Mt. Kehlstein. It is called the 'Eagle's Nest.' Hitler ascends to it in a lift quarried out of the heart of the mountain. It consists of two rooms only. One of them is a small kitchen, the other an enormous sitting-room of which every wall is of glass. Sitting in it must be rather like sitting in the centre of a bubble. Its furniture is simple. A desk, two or three divans, and a large telescope through which the Führer can peer. That is all. It is to this room that Hitler goes to brood. No telephone connects him with the outside world. He sits there sometimes for hours dreaming and planning new schemes of conquest. I believe only two foreigners have ever visited this hide-out—one was Unity Mitford, the other Count Ciano. I shall have more to say of the Mitford girl later.

There is some secret about this 'Eagle's Nest.' What it is I cannot say. It may be some mechanical device, planned to protect Hitler from attack if ever the almost impregnable house at Berchtesgaden is taken by his enemies. But whatever it is, one was never allowed to ask many questions about the method of its construction.

Some of Hitler's staff declared that the Führer planned to lie there after his death, as Lenin lies in the Red Square at Moscow. It is quite likely. It is the kind of thing that would appeal to his imagination. Now, of course, it is unlikely that his body will ever know such a resting-place.

This, then, is Berchtesgaden—the storm-centre of Europe.

And now what of the man whose home it is ? I have spoken to the Führer some half-dozen times. Once he talked to me for over half an hour. But I have seen him hundreds of times, have seen him with his friends, discussed him with his other servants, watched and studied him for many months. I feel I know him as few outside his small circle of friends can ever hope to know him. Now it is time the world should see him through my eyes.

CHAPTER THREE

ONE CURIOUS FICTION CURRENT IN EVERY foreign country is that Adolf Hitler has little interest in food. I can assure you that the kitchens at Berchtesgaden are probably the most carefully supervised and important rooms in the entire *ménage*.

It is true that the Führer is a vegetarian, but he is finicky to the point of obsession about what he eats and how it is served. Every morsel must be of the best and woe betide Otto Schlieben, head of the domestic staff, if it is not cooked to perfection. Four chefs are employèd in the kitchens. Every one came from a different famous Berlin restaurant. They are under the supervision of the only foreigner serving in Berchtesgaden. This man is Rudi Vanyor, a Hungarian. He got his job because he is the greatest authority on vegetarian food in Europe. He is now a German citizen and is paid a fabulous salary.

The Führer is a late riser, contrary to popular belief, and he never breakfasts before ten o'clock. Often it is eleven. He takes a simple meal, usually comprising a glass of orange juice, followed by a few slices of rye bread and butter.

Hermann Goering has said that Germans prefer guns to butter, but his Leader loves both. He usually gets through half a pound a day. Local farmers send supplies to the kitchens daily.

Lunch is Hitler's favourite meal. It begins invariably with vegetable soup, of which he manages to get through an incredible amount. The recipe may be worth putting on record. Here it is : Onion, celery, chopped parsley, potatoes, turnips, carrots, nut compound, slices of apple, flour, water and salt. Soup is followed by fish, for Hitler is not a true vegetarian but merely a non-meat eater. He has a passion for trout, served with a special butter sauce. *Sauté* potatoes usually accompany the fish.

Then a great bowl of assorted nuts comes to the table and the Führer simply stuffs himself with these.

He is not strictly teetotal, though near enough for all practical purposes. He never touches wines or spirits, but he does have an occasional glass of 'near beer,' which is much weaker even than light lager. I imagine one could drink quarts of this beer without experiencing the slightest alcoholic effect. Its chief resemblance to real beer is its colour.

Hitler drinks an enormous amount of coffee. And he loves it to be very black and very sweet. Sixteen cups a day, and they are big ones, make up his usual ration.

Dinner is the day's most elaborate meal at Berchtesgaden—but not for the Führer, oddly enough. Though the meal rarely has fewer than six courses, they are enjoyed only by the guests of the day. Hitler eats little at this time. More often than not he takes a small salad, potatoes cooked in one of a dozen different ways, and a sweet—of which he is very fond.

Long before he came to real power, Hitler used to visit the Kaiserhof or Adlon hotel in Berlin every afternoon and munch his way through a large plate of cream buns. These are his favourite sweets and they are on the menu at least four days a week.

Guests at dinner are permitted to drink wine provided it comes from German vineyards. This proviso has always irked Goering, who prides himself on being something of a connoisseur of wines and boasts a very fine cellar stocked with French and Italian wines at his own home, Karin Hall.

Smoking, of course, is absolutely taboo in Hitler's presence or even in any room he might enter. He loathes the smell of tobacco, and he has been known to snatch a cigarette from the lips of an unsuspecting guest enjoying a quiet smoke on one of the terraces when the Führer came across him.

As normal men smoke, Hitler eats sweets. He eats pounds of them a week. He is childishly fond of toffee and chocolate. A bag of sweetmeats is always in his jacket pocket. I once heard him declare to Goebbels: "They give me energy for my great tasks, Joseph." Another thing I discovered after a very short time at the Berghof was that the German Leader is the worst-dressed man in the land. Yet he has a private tailor, one Herr Andergruss. His clothes are always ill-fitting because he will not suffer to be properly measured or fitted, with the result that his tailor has to guess most of his measurements. Hitler is completely indifferent to clothes. For a supreme ruler he must have the world's smallest wardrobe. It consists of a few uniforms, five ordinary lounge suits and two suits of evening dress. And even these are the despair of his valet.

For one thing the patterns of the materials he chooses are dull and suburban. Black and dark grey are the only colours he tolerates in his civilian suits. He treats them badly, too, slouching in chairs, with legs bent so that his trousers always become baggy at the knees within an hour or two. Also, his pockets always bulge with bags of sweets or masses of papers. In fact, Hitler can be guaranteed to reduce the best-tailored suit to a shapeless collection of ill-fitting garments in a few days.

As a matter of fact, he regards interest in clothes as a weakness in men, and he never ceases taxing Goering with vanity because of that great man's notorious collection of uniforms.

Hitler has a sentimental affection for the simple uniform of the Storm Trooper—brown shirt, breeches, knee-high boots. It is the one uniform in which he himself feels at home.

The one great peculiarity of the Führer which causes most trouble to his immediate circle of colleagues and servants, however, is his insomnia. He sleeps extremely little. And it is his abiding curse.

It makes his time-table of daily work terribly difficult and exacting for ordinary folk. He rarely gets up before ten a.m., as we have seen, and he never does any work at all until after lunch. Even then, he usually spends the afternoon talking with political visitors or gossiping

D

with friends. He does little serious work. This begins when dinner is over at half past eight. Only then does the Führer go to his desk.

First, he studies a summary of news from the world's Press. This is prepared by a dozen linguistic experts who are called Press secretaries. They have a difficult task. It is not true, as I have seen in foreign newspapers, that Hitler's advisers, such as Ribbentrop and Goebbels, censor these news digests to keep from the Führer news they don't want him to know about. But the Press secretaries exercise a kind of censorship of their own—not for political reasons, but on the grounds of prudence. Hitler cannot bear humour at his expense. Cartoons in English and American papers send him into violent rages. So do the many satirical poems published abroad. The English cartoonist, Low, especially enrages the Führer.

Such things as these, therefore, are kept from him, for when he sees one he vents his rage on the unfortunate secretary who put it before him.

When he has assimilated the news, Hitler rings for his ordinary secretaries, who work in shifts, and begins to dictate. He does this at top speed and shouts as though he were addressing a public meeting. His phrasing and grammar are appallingly bad, and they have to be carefully edited before they appear on paper.

Hitler spends about an hour and a half dictating memoranda in the ordinary way. These are then despatched by wire or despatch rider to officials all over the country.

Hitler, by the way, is full of contempt for the freedom of opinion enjoyed by newspapers in other countries.

"The Governments of those countries are spineless," I have heard him say. "The Press exists to do as it is told, not to tell Governments what to do. To preserve a free Press is as sensible as preserving an ulcer. That is what a free Press is—an ulcer, an abscess on the body of the State."

After he has finished dictating, Hitler talks to his political and military advisers. Or rather he talks at them. He will not endure a word of criticism. Goering has come as near to that as anyone in Germany dare. But even he has to tread warily.

I was once serving coffee in the Führer's study when he was talking to Goering. Hitler was sitting at his desk and the fat Field-Marshal was pacing up and down when I entered. I cannot remember what they were talking about, but suddenly Goering stopped walking up and down, went up to the desk and declared : "You cannot do it. The whole idea is stupid."

Hitler instantly rose to his feet.

"What !" he shouted. "You dare to tell your Leader what he can and cannot do. You dare to say my ideas are stupid ? No one can advise me. I am supreme throughout the Reich. I, Adolf Hitler, rule this country. And what I say is law. Remember that, Hermann."

His voice had risen to a hysterical shriek before he finished, and when he sank back into his chair even the great Goering was a little shaken.

Hitler was silent for a few seconds, then he motioned to me to serve the coffee. I had been stock-still by the door during his tirade, not daring to move.

As he sipped his black coffee, the Führer went on talking in a normal voice again to Goering as though nothing had happened. But with people lower in the hierarchy than Goering this fury would last much longer. Often it would end with severe penalties, such as reduction in rank.

Hitler's after-dinner talks last far into the early hours of the morning. Several of his permanent entourage are good pianists, and when the Führer feels inspiration flag he makes one of them play for him. He loves Wagner and the sugary sentimental strains of a number of minor German and Austrian composers.

As he listens to the piano, he lies back in his chair, with his eyes closed and his fingers gently keeping time to the music. He hates jazz music or dance music. "Negroid perversions" is how he characterises almost any music from England or America. Often, when he has at last gone to bed, the Führer finds that sleep is still eluding him. Then he will get up, return to his study and have one of his guests roused for him—or her—to talk. Goebbels is nearly always unlucky in this respect when he is at Berchtesgaden.

He is dragged from bed to listen to vast propaganda schemes the Führer has devised in the small hours. Goebbels, with nodding head, has to sit there until dawn breaks over the Bavarian Alps. The kitchen, too, must be ever on the alert for orders to produce snacks or black coffee.

When Hitler is not in the mood for talking or reading, he will go for long night drives in one of his big black Mercédès tourers.

From my bedroom window I have often seen the car gliding out of the garage at midnight. He never drives himself. He is far too nervous. But he loves speed. His drivers have told me that on these nocturnal trips the speedometer rarely drops below sixty miles an hour, and often hits the hundred mark.

Hitler's favourite reading, apart from his never satisfied study of German history, is any book about the building of the British Empire. Clive, Wolfe, Drake, and men like these seem to be his heroes. He is Britain's greatest admirer, though he displays such contempt for her in public.

Experts from all over the world have been called in to cure the Führer's insomnia, but none has ever succeeded. He will not submit to any kind of drugs. When the real doctors were baffled he turned child-like to the quacks. Whenever an item about a cure for insomnia appears in a newspaper, the professed magician is summoned to Germany, no matter whether he lives in India or China, and paid an enormous fee to try his skill on Hitler. Perhaps the most fantastic cure he tried was undertaken at the suggestion of a famous Swiss psychologist.

A cinema screen was fitted to the ceiling of Hitler's bedroom and from a concealed projector the coloured moving picture of a waterfall was thrown on to it. The

Führer was told to make his mind a blank and to gaze steadily at the falling water. He tried this for nearly a fortnight, during which millions of gallons of cinematic water must have fallen past his staring eyes, before the cure was abandoned as hopeless. On another occasion a Viennese specialist persuaded him that a series of exercises would prove efficacious, and for a week or two the Führer was performing contortions in his bedroom, one of which included standing on his head, I was told, so that the blood would rush to his brain, and then standing upright so that the blood would drain away rapidly. This was the best joke of his entourage while it lasted, though, of course, no hint of the fun was allowed to reach the Führer's ears.

Hitler takes extraordinary precautions to protect himself from enemies, apart from the normal protection of armed guards and bullet-proof guards.

He is terrified of being poisoned. No one in his own household, even, is above suspicion.

Samples of all his food are taken by a staff of analytical chemists and carefully examined hours before the food is served. Hitler does not believe in having a food-taster in case a very slow poison might be used on him. The raw materials of the kitchen are examined by the chemists. And only the four chefs are allowed afterwards to touch the food or the dishes.

Another precaution Hitler takes is the wearing of a bullet-proof vest. He dons this whenever he leaves the house. It can often be seen bulging through his coat in pictures. It is made of leather and a special light steel alloy, and is proof against the most powerful bullet in the world.

There are whispers that twice already it has saved his life, but I do not know whether this is true.

In his relations with the domestic staff, Hitler is a curious mixture. Sometimes he will ignore their existence. He has a trick of appearing unaware of you in his presence which is very disconcerting. At other times, he gets into rages over trivialities such as the way his room has been tidied or as the amount of coffee served to him.

On these occasions he can work himself into as great a fury as he does over political issues of the highest importance. He has even been known to fall into one of his notorious fits of hysterical weeping because a servant has upset him in some utterly trifling way. He will then accuse the offender of trying to distract him from his vital task of rebuilding the Reich, and it may mean the concentration-camp if the usual reaction of forgiveness does not set in quickly.

But there are also times when Hitler treats his servants almost as equals. Then he will tell them that all are comrades in the common task and that his cooks are doing their bit as much as his generals.

Hitler is often in such a mood after he has pulled off a big coup. Then he may give his servants presents. I once received from him, to my astonishment, a thousand-mark note when I entered his study to serve a meal at his desk.

He smiled at me, told me I was pretty, and thrust the note into my hand "as a reward for faithful service, Fräulein." (I was not allowed the status of marriage at the Berghof.)

Hitler has all the normal man's liking for a pretty face and a trim figure, though he dislikes women to use make-up or to be attractive in an artificial way.

Pretty women, as I shall show later, play an important part in the Führer's life at Berchtesgaden. He never gives a party without half a dozen of them in evidence. Hitler's parties are not very popular with his guests, largely because of the restrictions on smoking and drinking and his predilection for the same type of music which is played eternally to the victims.

But, of course, no one dares to refuse an invitation.

It is amusing for the domestic staff to watch the guests one at a time disappear when the Führer does not notice to smoke or to get a drink in another part of the house. Usually they go to the quarters of the Black Guard officers to find good company and amusement.

Sometimes one of them is suddenly missed by the Führer, and he will send servants to find them and reproach them for leaving without his permission.

Even conversation is restricted at these parties. Hitler cannot bear joking, particularly jokes that sail too near the political wind. And since few guests have the status or courage to attempt to lead the conversation the parties are really nothing but informal political meetings gathered to listen to the Leader. The women, particularly, find this boring, but as they have always the axe of a husband or lover to grind they form an adoring audience which seems to take the Führer in completely, for he is always pleased when the women compliment him on his political acumen.

I have already mentioned the rules drawn up for servants at Berchtesgaden. Guests who stay there also have to study a set of rules which they find on their dressing-tables. I still have a copy of these rules which I smuggled out when I left. They are worth reproducing here.

INSTRUCTIONS TO VISITORS

1. Smoking is forbidden except in this bedroom.
2. The guest must not talk to servants or carry any parcel or message from the premises for any servant.
3. At all times the Führer must be addressed and spoken of as such and never as 'Herr Hitler' or other title.
4. Women guests are forbidden to use excessive cosmetics and must on no account use colouring material on their finger-nails.
5. Guests must present themselves for meals within two minutes of the announcing bell. No one may sit at table or leave the table until the Führer has sat or left.
6. No one may remain seated in a room when the Führer enters.
7. Guests must retire to their rooms at eleven p.m. unless expressly asked to remain by the Führer.

8. Guests must remain in this wing of the house and must on no account enter the domestic quarters, the offices or the quarters of the S.S. officers or the political police bureau.

9. On leaving Berchtesgaden, guests are absolutely forbidden to discuss their visit with strangers or to mention any remark made to them by the Führer. The conveying of information about the Führer's private life in this way will be visited by the severest penalties.

Probably more fantastic stories of Hitler's health than of any other aspect of the Führer's life have been circulated round the world. Never a week passes without a foreign newspaper printing prominently an 'authoritative' tale of Hitler's illness, physical or mental.

These stories infuriate the Führer almost as much as the foreign cartoons. They are more irritating to him because they are all based on truth.

Hitler's health is very bad. I do not pretend to be able to reveal guaranteed accurate information about it, because the subject is one which the Führer keeps from even his closest associates. The only other people who could tell the whole story are the famous German heart and throat specialist, Professor Sauerbruch, who has operated on Hitler three times, Professor Knoll, the great Berlin physician, who is the Führer's permanent doctor, and Professor Henry Steinmetz.

Many other specialists of many capitals, including Paris and New York, have been to Berchtesgaden. But all have kept their secret well.

But I can reveal one or two facts which I gleaned from Franz Wrabel, Hitler's valet, and Elsa Holzfahn, the assistant housekeeper, who enjoys the confidence of Paula Hitler, the Führer's sister.

Hitler's heart has caused great anxiety. His throat has been attacked by a cancerous growth.

When Professor Sauerbruch operated on Hitler the first time it was announced that he had removed a polypus from the right vocal chord. It was not announced that a second and a third operation were necessary within a short time. Stories of voice strain due to over-speaking in public could not account for this. The story I was told by Elsa Holzfahn could account for it.

SHE TOLD ME THAT IN REMOVING A CANCEROUS GROWTH FROM THE VOCAL CHORD THE CHORD WAS DESTROYED AND THAT AN ARTIFICIAL CHORD MADE FROM STRIPS OF THE FÜHRER'S OWN SKIN WAS GRAFTED INTO THE THROAT TO REPLACE IT.

It is now believed that the cancer danger has been removed and that Sauerbruch's brilliant operation saved the Führer's voice, though it can never be anything but hoarse and harsh in the future.

I do know that Sauerbruch wanted to call in the Viennese surgeon Professor Neumann, who operated on the Duke of Windsor, but that the Führer refused to permit this because Neumann is a Jew. The Führer is extremely susceptible to colds, and it was for this reason that his own specialist wanted to call in the Viennese, apart from the vocal chord trouble.

At one period the Führer's heart was constantly letting him down. He would have to rest for days at a time, doing nothing, often when he had tasks of the greatest urgency. He has what is called a tired heart, and the great strain he continually puts upon it is the despair of Professor Knoll.

Frequently, when he should rest and refuses to do so, the doctors resort to injections of stimulants, sometimes several times a day. These are temporary measures which are actually doing him harm, but there is no other way out.

Bouts of illness always make the Führer gloomy and angry. It is always hard on his colleagues at these times. He is also liable to refer to his approaching end in public speeches, though he does not seem to be afraid of dying.

One thing he cannot bear is sickness in others. He has no patience with it and will never see anyone who is ill, even a close friend. Signs of illness at Berchtesgaden must be rigorously kept from his sight.

He has little respect for his own doctors and treats Knoll like a waiter. Perhaps it is that in the presence of such men that he loses that great sense of being a superman and feels that he is helpless in their hands. His treatment of the doctors by way of 'revenge' is not explicable in any other way.

There is one amusing example of his childishness in this respect. Whenever he has to take medicine or to be injected with any substance he insists on the doctors taking the medicine or submitting to the needle themselves first.

He also seems to find amusement in setting the doctors to work on his friends.

He enrages Goering by insisting that he shall submit to diet and weight-reducing cures. These rarely have any effect on the great Hermann (probably because he breaks the rules on the sly, for he is a great gourmet and wine-bibber), and Hitler will then taunt the medicos with their inability.

Hitler has all the average man's horror of the dentist, and he is unfortunately quite often in that individual's hands. His dentist is the Berlin expert Hartenstein. He has great difficulty with the august patient, who screams with pain like any little boy when an extraction hurts a little. Yet Hitler will not have gas. He is terrified of anæsthetics. Only for a very serious operation would he permit it.

It is little known that the Führer has eight false teeth and has a number of gold fillings.

Another aspect of the Führer's life which provides scope for fantastic stories all over the world is his employment of doubles to appear for him in public on suitable occasions.

There are three Hitler doubles. No one but the Gestapo, who, with amazing efficiency, found them, know their names.

At close quarters, it is quite simple to differentiate

between them, but when they are dressed in Hitler clothes and touched up by make-up experts it is impossible to tell them from the Führer at twenty yards' distance. Only one of these men, however, has a voice like Hitler. In his case a natural similarity was carefully developed until he was trained to make short speeches in the Führer's stead on unimportant occasions.

One of the doubles is always at Berchtesgaden, another at Munich, and the third in Berlin, ready to proceed to any part of Germany or Austria at a moment's notice.

The chief task of the doubles is to stand-in for the Führer for street processions, military reviews or similar occasions on which speech is unnecessary, but also on which the danger of assassination is ever present.

Not always is the same double stationed at Berchtesgaden. The three take it in turns to stand by there, for there is rarely need for them in the Führer's retreat, and it is considered a very cushy spell of duty. They are known by various nicknames at the Berghof, usually 'One,' 'Two' and 'Three.' Also 'Little Willi,' 'Old Bismarck,' and 'Putzi.'

They live in the S.S. quarters and have no rank or authority. Nearly everyone treats them with a kind of amused contempt. Only one of them, Putzi, has ever been attacked in mistake for his master.

He was shot in the shoulder at a review of Brownshirts in the Maximilian-strasse at Munich. The bullet was fired from the direction of the National Theatre from a gun fitted with silencer, and no one but Himmler and Goering, who were in the car with Putzi as it crawled past the ranks of Storm Troopers, ever knew that an attempt had been made on 'the Führer.' Putzi was not badly hurt and he went through the ceremony without flinching. The gun-man was never caught. The story was never revealed to the world.

Putzi was taken back to Hitler's flat in Munich and doctored. When he was better he was given a bonus of 5,000 marks and a holiday.

Once a mistake was made in sending a double to Frankfort when Hitler himself was visiting his Gauleiter for Bavaria. This was due to a mistake by the Gestapo men at Berchtesgaden, but it was also due to the fact that Hitler had made a sudden change of plans and no one had realized that the double was scheduled to visit Frankfort.

The embarrassing result was that early editions of newspapers in Frankfort and Munich carried stories that the Führer had made public appearances at both places at the same time. All possible editions of the papers were recalled, but hundreds must have reached the public before the Gestapo realized what had happened. Three high Gestapo officials were severely punished for this bad piece of blundering. One of them was dismissed from the service.

I liked Little Willi best of all the doubles. He had a real sense of humour and he used to fraternise with us servants, often playing cards with us in our recreation room. He was also a marvellous table-tennis player and could beat everyone in the house at this game, which is very popular at Berchtesgaden. I often tried to persuade him to tell me his real name, where he came from, and how he was picked up by the Gestapo. But the subject was *verboten* and the surveillance of the secret police so efficient and dreaded that I could never draw him out. I was rather sorry for Little Willi—in fact, for all the doubles, because they are cut off from the world. They will never see their friends or relatives again. They know it. Willi was also very much in love with Emma Klatz, one of the maids. She loved him too. But, of course, they knew that they could never marry or escape. They snatched what happiness they could in secret whenever he was stationed at Berghof. Emma was always terrified when he went away on a job. She feared he would be killed one day.

Four maids take it in turns of a week at a time to look after the Führer's bedroom. While they are in the room they are always under the watchful eyes of Franz, the valet.

The room is very plainly furnished with a large iron-framed bed, a small side-table, a larger table by the big window, an easy chair and a desk over which a small bookshelf runs. A small dressing-room adjoins.

The bed is covered with a great brown quilt embroidered with a huge swastika. The Führer, by the way, wears surprisingly (for him) luxurious pyjamas. They are brown satin with darker brown cuffs and lapels. A swastika in black on a red background is embroidered on the pocket.

He has a heavy silk dressing-gown in similar colours.

A small writing-pad and a pencil always lie on the little table at the bedside. Usually, the used sheets were torn off by the Führer or by Franz every morning, but one day when I was tidying up the room I saw a crumpled sheet lying beside the waste-paper basket as though it had been aimed at the basket but had fallen on the floor unnoticed. I quickly picked it up while Franz was not looking and put it in my pocket. I was curious to see what Hitler scribbled during his sleepless nights.

I did not look at it again until I was in my room. It seemed like a rough map of the district. Names of people were scribbled all over it. And there were a lot of meaningless scrawls such as one makes unconsciously while concentrating. I could make nothing of it, but I put it away in a drawer as a memento.

Two days later it happened that I had to go before the Gestapo for my monthly report. This is made out for every servant by Otto Schlieben rather in the manner of a school report. Each servant gets marks for efficiency, neatness, discretion, and bad marks for mistakes, break-ages, complaints, etc. To have a bad mark as a result of even the most trifling complaint from Hitler entails loss of salary for a month and confinement to the house during that period.

On this particular occasion I had quite a clear conscience and I was quite undisturbed when I stood before the desk of the Gestapo officer-in-charge, one Fritz Glass.

He went through each item on the report in the usual

way and said pleasantly : "An excellent report, Fräulein."

I smiled and thanked him. Then he said in the same pleasant tone : "Have you nothing on your conscience, my dear ? Nothing that the good Schlieben has overlooked ?"

I was startled, but I could honestly think of nothing, and I said so quite firmly. Then, sharply :

"Where is the piece of paper you took from the Führer's bedroom, Fraulein ?"

My heart leapt. I blushed madly. I stammered. I knew I had been caught, but I could not imagine how. Glass informed me. It was a trap to test me. The paper had been left there deliberately. I tried to explain lamely that I thought it was a piece of waste-paper and that I had meant to burn it. But my story was a poor one and I knew it. I was sent to my room and told to stay there until further orders pending a decision on my punishment. I was terrified as I sat alone. But even in my fear I could not help admiring the efficiency of the Gestapo. They overlook nothing and they never take a chance.

In the evening I was sent for by Schlieben to hear my fate. I was very lucky. My sentence was loss of pay for three months and confinement to the house for one. My light sentence was due to the fact that I had never previously been an offender and that my record was regarded as very good. Also, I think, I was pretty popular with Schlieben, the assistant housekeeper, Elsa, and, as a matter of fact, with most of the Gestapo men. Of course, I was given as well a very sound wigging and a warning that the concentration-camp would inevitably follow the next mistake of the same kind.

I never allowed my curiosity to get me into trouble again. Life went uneventfully for a while. I was quite happy at the Berghof. True, we could never leave the grounds but the gardens are beautiful and we had plenty of exercise. Also we had our recreations and our friendships and we had the best food in Germany, which is more important than most foreigners will be able to understand.

On rare occasions we were taken for motor-drives round the district, but we were never allowed to leave the cars. The only permanent cloud on the horizon was my ignorance of what had happened to my husband and to my parents. I tried repeatedly to find out from the Gestapo, but they were never able or they were not willing to help me.

The Gestapo squad at Berchtesgaden was changed every three months, but I had always found them pleasant enough when I was on their side of the fence, and I had almost lost my terror of the most dreaded organization in Germany.

One day Himmler made a new appointment. He sent one of his lieutenants, Gregor Hausmann, to become a semi-permanent representative at the Berghof. Hausmann was Goering-like in girth and had a neck that burst in folds over his uniform collar. He was not, unluckily, as convivial as the Field-Marshal, however. He began a minor reign of terror among the servants. One of his first acts was to search the room of every one of us with real Gestapo throughness. He punished the most venial offence with the severest penalties and before long he had everyone shaking in his shoes.

He also took over the duty of examining Schlieben's monthly reports. And what used to be little more than a formality became an occasion which everyone of us dreaded days beforehand. One day when I was before him I was surprised to find him unusually pleasant. "You have a very good record here, Fräulein," he said. And he picked up my hand in his fat paw. "We could do with more servants as excellent as you—and as pretty."

He leered in a way which was no doubt intended to be pleasant, but which made me shudder. He had a repellent face. I sensed what was coming with despair, and I resolved to defy Hausmann. I felt strong enough to report him to Schlieben or Elsa and I knew that it would go hard with him if I were believed. Then my hopes and confidence crashed. The fat official said smoothly :

"I see, though, that there is one blot on your record. Conviction of theft from the Führer's bedroom. That is very serious, Fräulein. You know what another slip would mean. I hope you are going to step carefully in future. It would be a pity if we had to lose you."

I knew then that I could never oppose this man. It would have been too easy for him to frame up another serious charge against me and then no one would be able to save me. And I was determined never to see the inside of another Dachau whatever the cost. I was sick with fear, but I managed to say meekly: "No, Herr Hausmann, I shall not offend again."

To my surprise he dismissed me with a smile, and I breathed a sigh of relief as I scuttled back to my quarters. The respite was only temporary.

Two nights later I was on late duty in the kitchen when one of the phones from the bedrooms rang. Schlieben was on duty, too, as it happened and he answered the phone. He listened for a few moments and then said : "Yes, Herr Hausmann."

He looked at me curiously and said : "Coffee and sandwiches for Herr Hausmann, Fraulein."

I think he guessed from the dismay on my face what was in the wind, but Hausmann was a power and Otto was not going to be curious.

I filled a tray and went up in the lift to Hausmann's room with my heart pounding and a strange sinking sensation in my stomach. I hated all men. I cursed my pretty face. I wished I had been born fat or ugly or deformed.

I knocked at the door of the bedroom. A harsh voice bade me enter. Hausmann was sitting propped up in bed reading. He had a pair of thick horn-rimmed spectacles on. He wore pale blue silk pyjamas through which his rolls of fat bulged tightly. He seemed more gross than ever without his uniform which held him together a little. I almost wanted to laugh at the creature.

"Ah, coffee, my dear. Excellent." He beamed. "Put

it down here, Fräulein." He patted the side-table with a fat paw.

As I stooped and deposited the tray he took hold of my arm, gently but firmly, and grinned: "Stay awhile—Pauline. I want to talk to you. Tell me more about yourself and your life. I like you. You are an intelligent girl and I might be able to do something for you one day. Those hands deserve a better fate than domestic work."

I began to talk about my life at home and in the laundry at Karlsruhe, and as I spoke, Hausmann was nodding approvingly and emitting little grunts. But his eyes were not on my face. They were on my ankles and my breasts. I felt that he was caressing me mentally. I was trembling.

"Sit down here, Pauline," he commanded, and I sat tensely on the edge of the bed. He put an arm round my waist and pulled me a little closer.

"I think I should be returning to the kitchen, sir," I ventured, "Herr Schlieben may miss me and I may be needed."

Hausmann smiled. "I don't think Herr Schlieben will worry," he replied. And then I guessed what had been spoken over the phone in the kitchen.

"Don't you like me, Pauline," asked the man whose very presence made me want to vomit.

I smiled feebly. "Of course, Herr Hausmann."

One fat hand began to stroke my knee. I felt it, hot, on my thigh. It was like being a mouse in the claws of a cat. Suddenly, I was jerked violently face down over the man and his eyes blazed with lust. He began to undress me. When I was almost naked save for my brassiere and my knickers he threw back the bedclothes and pulled me under them with him. He removed his own pyjama coat and I noticed with an odd feeling of complete detachment that he had tufts of black hair growing from his chest. His breasts were bigger than many women's. They hung against his fat-covered ribs like bags of dough.

E

One arm like a thigh went up in the air. There was a click, and we were in the dark . . . .

That was the beginning of the six most unpleasant months I spent at the Berghof. I became Hausmann's mistress. Everyone knew of it, but of course they imagined I was quite a willing party—except my intimate friends.

Decency forbids me to record the bestiality of the man and the things he compelled me to do during those six months.

Once, I thought I was going to have a child and I told him so. He was furious. He secured some pills which contained what I do not know. The danger passed. To my relief as well as his. I think I should have strangled a child from that creature. After six months he was called away from Berchtesgaden and he never returned, to my unbounded delight.

He was replaced by a much younger and pleasanter man, Captain Rinz, who was never anything but charming to all of us. After all, the Gestapo men felt themselves to be rather above having domestics as mistresses. They were allowed to bring their own women to the Berghof. And their taste usually ran to actresses from Munich or Berlin or to the wives and daughters of the upper classes who were seeking their favours.

Of course, there were real affairs among the domestics. Two of my friends, Greta Fursch and Karen Pfeifer, were the mistresses of two of the gardeners. They were all very much in love. Even Schlieben, whom I regarded as an old man, carried on a romance with one of the girls who seemed genuinely to have an affection for him, though how anyone could love a man with a face like his patched-up one I could never imagine.

I suppose the virtual imprisonment at Berchtesgaden had the effect of creating a desire for the opposite sex as real imprisonment does, though this is quenched in the German prisons by the regular administration of anaphrodisiacs in food. Personally, I never had any such desire. My experiences had given me an aversion from sex relationship from which I have never really recovered.

I have seen too much of the barbaric, beastly side of men who have dropped the mask that a few thousand years of civilization has given them. I believe that all men are capable of this kind of excess and savagery, but that some are able to keep it under control wholly or partly.

I have not mentioned one unusual fact about life at the Berghof. There are no wireless sets. That is, for the use of the staff. Hitler has two powerful sets, each capable of receiving any station in the world. There are also sets in the Gestapo offices—and a transmitter.

But the use of radio sets by servants or staff for private pleasure is not allowed. We were not even permitted to hear the German stations on the special people's set with its limited reception powers. I do not know the reason for this rule but I was told that it was to keep us in ignorance of events outside in case we ever panicked in the event of a crisis like an armed rising and might be tempted to help the rebels from inside. It seemed a poor reason to me, but there is the fact.

Because of this we were allowed to get up shows of our own or occasionally to be visited by a sort of concert party or a team of actors performing popular plays.

These shows always took place in the big recreation room which was fitted with a proper stage.

We had great fun in producing shows, and I found that I had a talent for singing. I nearly always had an important part in every show we did ourselves. The Gestapo men, the Storm Troopers and the outside staff as well as the servants were allowed to attend or to take part.

Goering watched the performances several times and once Hitler himself paid us a surprise visit, much to the confusion of some of the cast who forgot their lines on the stage and had to be prompted in loud whispers which made everyone, including Hitler, roar with laughter.

I was quite cool, however, and I was afterwards

complimented by the Führer on my singing. I was tremendously pleased and I was the envy of everybody in the show. I think it was not so much my voice as the song I sang that pleased the Führer. It was "Vilia", from the *Merry Widow* and one of Hitler's favourite songs.

Ever afterwards I was the star of the shows we put on, except when a play was performed, which was not often.

Of course, we enjoyed the professional players' shows, too. Our favourite was Viktor Skubl, the Berlin comedian, who brought several shows to Berchtesgaden before he was banned from the stage by Goebbels for making jokes in a Berlin night-club about the regime. We never saw him after that. I believe he was actually sent to a concentration camp.

I became quite wealthy after two years as Hitler's maid. For one thing the salary was very high for a domestic servant, and for another, it was quite impossible to spend it all. Our uniforms were provided, of course, as well as stockings and shoes, and even underwear.

We made various little personal purchases which we had to put on a list once a month to be fetched from shops in town by Gestapo men when they drove in.

We had to contribute ten per cent of our earnings to the Nazi Party and we had to subscribe generously to the Winter Relief Fund and to other Party-organized 'charities'.

Still, I found that I had 3,000 marks saved up which was more money than I had ever seen in my life. I had no idea what to do with it. I often wondered whether I should ever get out of Berchtesgaden before the Nazi régime cracked and disappeared as I knew in my heart it would one day. I weighed up my chances of escape in the event of, say, revolution. Would anyone believe I was anything but a Nazi? Worse, would Berchtesgaden be left standing, or would it be bombed and shelled with a Hitler, defiant to the end, dead among its ruins along with his staff?

I often dreamed of escaping to England or to America. It seemed impossible that I should get away.

I had only seen two changes on the staff since I had been at the Berghof. Both were girls who had been dismissed and sent to a concentration-camp. They were replaced. I wondered if anyone could leave in the normal way and get back to normal life if one schemed a little. I asked Schlieben about this. But he only asked in return : "Are you not satisfied to serve the Führer, Fräulein ?"

I hurriedly affirmed my loyalty and stopped asking questions. But the idea remained in my mind and I became more and more determined to make an effort to get away without, of course, risking Dachau again. It was many, many months before I found out how to do it.

Chapter Four

THERE WERE ALWAYS VISITORS COMING AND going. I saw most of them. Some were old friends of Hitler's, now given a minor rank in the Nazi hierarchy, others were world-famous figures. There was never a day without someone. For Hitler detests being alone, except for the few hours he spends in his retreat on Mount Kehlstein or dabbling in the occult. He must have people around him provided, of course, that they agree with him and are prepared to listen to his tirades.

There is one visitor I shall never forget. I doubt if the outside world will ever be allowed to see him again. I am speaking of Schuschnigg, the Chancellor of Austria. He came and went away a broken, beaten man.

It was in January 1938 that I first realized that Hitler meant to invade Austria. On January 26th, the Austrian police raided an office in the Teinfaltstrasse in Vienna. There they found a document signed 'R.H.' In great detail it outlined a plan by which the Nazis hoped to conquer Austria. Austrian Nazis, helped by their German comrades, were to stir up trouble throughout Austria. There were to be riots and demonstrations and, after a few days, the German Reichswehr were to cross the frontier to 'restore order.'

But the moment this plan was discovered all the Nazi leaders in Austria were arrested.

I knew something was in the wind on the morning of January 27th. Cars kept arriving at Berchtesgaden every few minutes. Hess arrived, looking shaken, for the initials 'R.H.' were his. Hitler held conference all that day and far into the early hours of the next morning.

Naturally I heard nothing of what was decided. But I soon saw. For on February 6th, von Papen, Nazi

Ambassador in Vienna, arrived at Berchtesgaden and saw Hitler at once. He left again for Vienna as the bearer of an invitation to Schuschnigg to come to Berchtesgaden. And on February 11th Schuschnigg arrived. The day before had seen great activity. A crowd of important people descended on Berchtesgaden from Berlin. The ante-room of Hitler's study was given special attention. I know because I worked in it all day. Most of the furniture was removed and a great table placed in the centre of the floor. On it was spread a large-scale map of Austria and southern Germany. Blood-red arrows were inked on it showing the route German troops would take if they invaded Austria. A model of a German bomber, complete in every detail, stood on a side-table. A deep fresco ran round the walls. It was made of pictures of the devastation caused by bombs in Guernica, in Barcelona, and in Madrid.

Schuschnigg was met by no guard of honour. Two extremely tough-looking S.S. men were his reception-ists. They informed him bluntly that they had orders to search him before allowing him into the Führer's presence. Schuschnigg flushed but decided it would be wiser to submit. He was then taken into this ante-room and left there alone. He was there for over an hour with an armed guard standing outside the door.

Then, without warning or announcement, several Austrians burst into the room. They were prominent members of the Austrian Nazi Party who had escaped to Germany. Their job was to insult their Chancellor. They did it thoroughly and it was not until he had had to listen to them for nearly twenty-minutes that he was allowed to step into Hitler's study. He did not find the Führer alone. Hitler was standing before the fire. Round him were General von Reichenau, the Nazi Army Commander in Leipzig, General Keitel, then just appointed Commander of the German Army, and General Sperrle, the Air Force Commander of Munich. Four members of the S.S. stood in corners of the room with drawn revolvers. It is to one of those men that I owe my knowledge of what happened during this fatal interview.

"So you've come!" snapped Hitler. "Sit down!"

Startled by the abruptness of this greeting, Schuschnigg dropped into a chair, pulled out his cigarette-case, and prepared to light a cigarette.

"Put that away," ordered Hitler. "The matter you are here about is too serious for smoking."

And throughout the hours of the interview which followed, the Austrian Chancellor, a very heavy smoker, was not allowed a single cigarette.

Hitler burst into one of his tirades. "Austria must be free," he shouted. "It is a German state. Providence has made me leader of the Reich, leader of all Germans. I am destined to drag Austria from the chaos in which she now finds herself. And you, Herr von Schuschnigg, imagine you can check my will and the will of Austria to return to the Reich. You are mistaken. Tell him what is to happen if he remains obstinate."

He turned to his military chiefs. In cold, determined voices they spoke of the German divisions waiting on the Austrian frontier and of the 300 bombers waiting to take off for Vienna. "We can," they said, "either take control of Austria without violence or with violence. If you, as Chancellor, choose violence Vienna will be razed to the ground. The choice is yours."

When they had finished, lunch was served, Hitler grew more human. He spoke to Schuschnigg in an almost friendly tone—but that did not last long.

The moment lunch was over, he began again, threatening and bullying. He made outrageous demands, saying that Austrian Nazis, who were plotting the destruction of Austria, should have full equality with other Austrians. They must be equally represented in the Government.

His face went white with passion. Every time Schuschnigg tried to speak, Hitler's voice rose to a scream and silenced him.

And in the end, after eleven hours of this, Schuschnigg had to agree and Hitler promised to preserve Austria's independence. But on one thing Schuschnigg stood firm. Hitler demanded that Seyss-Inquart, leader of the Austrian Nazis, should be made Minister of the Interior. Schuschnigg, however, said that he could not promise this until he had consulted Miklas, President of Austria. And nothing could make him budge from this attitude. So Hitler let him go and, like a defeated general, Schuschnigg drove away.

He nearly drove to his death, for—and this has until now been a closely kept secret—Hitler had made elaborate plans to murder the Chancellor if it suited his purpose.

Three Austrians who had fled from Austria to find protection with the Führer were involved in this plot, a plot which would have had greater repercussions than the Reichstag fire. I only discovered the name of one of them—Julius Weber. He had served a five-year sentence in an Austrian jail for robbery with violence and after his release had become a fanatical Nazi. Shortly before Schuschnigg's visit he and his two associates had been put through a rigorous drill with sub-machine guns and hand-grenades. They became extremely proficient in their use and were finally turned into efficient gangsters.

About five miles from Berchtesgaden, on the road along which Schuschnigg would have to travel on his return, is a little wood, hardly more than a copse. Here the three men were stationed on the day of the Chancellor's visit, all armed with their sub-machine-guns and hand-grenades. Fastened to a tree-trunk behind which they stood was a small red electric bulb, connected with a small button on Hitler's desk. Their eyes never left it. When it glowed red they would have known Hitler had given the signal for them to hurl their grenades at Schuschnigg's car and, if he should escape the explosion, riddle him with bullets.

There is no doubt that if Schuschnigg had remained intractable the signal would have been given and, instead of having to endure the horrors of imprisonment under the care of the Gestapo, he would have been murdered. It might have been better that way. Immediately they were satisfied Schuschnigg was dead the three of them were to give themselves up to the German police and declare that they had acted as Austrian patriots unable any longer to tolerate Schuschnigg's mismanagement of his country. Then they were to be tried—at a trial that would, of course, have enjoyed wide-world publicity. After a sentence of life-imprisonment, they would be secretly released.

At least, that was Hitler's promise, but I imagine they would have been secretly shot. Hitler would never have allowed them to live with such a secret in their hearts. But, as it happened, Hitler decided there was no need for Schuschnigg's murder.

Another constant visitor at Berchtesgaden was Hermann Goering, fat, red-faced, blue-eyed gangster. But a jovial gangster. I never saw him in a bad temper. He was always cracking jokes. Coarse and obscene as most of them were, it was still a relief to discover someone who had kept his sense of humour. Goering drinks a tremendous amount—beer and hock, chiefly, although he likes cognac, too. Time and time again he has arrived for a conference with the Führer dead-drunk and has had to be taken hurriedly away for medical treatment in an attempt to sober him up as quickly as possible.

His appetite is enormous. Whatever restrictions were imposed on the German people's food-supplies they never affected Goering's table. I have known him eat six eggs for breakfast, follow them with two pickled herrings and a dish of sauerkraut, and wash the whole lot down with a quart of beer.

His dinners are tremendous. He goes on eating long after everyone else has left the table. This amuses Hitler who often says that "little Hermann must keep his strength up."

There has been a lot of nonsense written about Goering's uniforms. He has no more than many other Nazi leaders. Actually his favourite suits are ordinary blue, faintly pin-striped lounge suits. He is careful, too, about his tailoring. Whatever he wears fits his vast bulk perfectly. The first time I saw him he weighed just under twenty stones. He was worried about it and went down to the kitchens himself to talk with the cooks and see if they could not provide him with food, large in bulk but non-fattening. At one time he was losing a pound of weight each week and was as happy as a child about it.

He used to tell everybody—Hitler and the servants included—just how much he weighed and just how fast his weight was going down.

Goering is not a religious man. He has always supported the paganism of the Third Reich. But one of his staff told me that he wears a small gold cross hanging from a chain round his bull-neck and that he never takes it off night or day. He was once asked about it. He flushed with anger and roughly told the questioner to mind his own business. It may have some religious significance for the second man in the Reich or it may be some sentimental relic. For Goering is sentimental. He has the brutality of the Prussian officer and can, when necessary, be completely ruthless. But a really genuine appeal to Goering usually produces results.

I remember one case in particular. A young man aged twenty had been sent to a concentration-camp for some remark against the régime. He was the only son of his widowed mother. He arrived in the camp a fortnight before Christmas. A week before Christmas his mother wrote a pathetic letter to Goering, saying that this would be the first Christmas her son had spent away from home, that he was really a good boy but a little rash in his speech. Could he help her ?

Now Goering insists on looking at all letters addressed to him. He read this and at once phoned through to the camp commander ordering the lad's immediate release. And for Christmas he sent an enormous goose and three bottles of cognac to the widow with a personal note. "Best wishes for Christmas. But tell your boy to think before he speaks next time."

Goering has a passion for toy-trains. His country home has one huge room fitted up with a network of railway lines on which superb models of trains run past miniature stations, through tunnels, and across bridges. He was always bringing photographs of this room to Berchtesgaden and discussing mechanical points with the various mechanics on the staff.

Hitler hates being touched. He only shakes hands when a ceremonious occasion demands it. But Goering slaps him on the back—and I think Hitler likes it. For, in spite of their quarrels, the Führer is very fond of Goering He respects Himmler, but has a real affection for Goering. Perhaps it is because Goering refuses to be bullied.

Goering is a magnificent shot. His hunting-parties are famous. He loves shooting, though, quite apart from hunting. When the Third Reich crashes Goering, if he is left alive, could always earn a good living in the music-halls as a trick revolver shot. He has often displayed his prowess in the gardens of Berchtesgaden.

He uses a .45 calibre six-shooter and his favourite trick is to stand six empty bottles on the ground thirty yards away from him. A marble is placed on the mouth of each bottle and Goering shatters each marble without touching the bottles.

And he is a good conjurer. He once wandered down to the servants' quarters and performed some astonishing tricks.

But it would be unfair to think of him as only a rather crude buffoon. He works very hard, but seems to be able to get through a great deal without apparent effort. He is a man of quick decisions, able to say 'yes' or 'no' to any problem almost instantly. His staff are devoted to him, largely because he often takes the blame for their mistakes.

I have heard Hitler raging at the incompetence of some minor officials and Goering quietly tell him that he himself ordered them to do the job in that way. Then, more often than not, Hitler's rage would subside and that would be the end of the matter.

In spite of their rows, I think there has only been one serious dispute between Hitler and Goering. It happened long before my time at Berchtesgaden. A woman was the cause of it. Rumours began to spread in Berlin and seep through to the provinces that Goering was very friendly with an actress and that the friendship had long since ceased to be platonic. The name of the actress was Emmy Sonnemann, a buxom blonde, with a bad voice and a poor figure, but a woman known throughout Germany for her many and colourful love affairs. Goering was the latest of her lovers. He bought her a little villa in Dahlem, a fashionable Berlin suburb, and spent many week-ends there.

About this time the Nazis were posing as puritans. Hitler heard about this affair and was furious. What was the good of exhorting Germans to be pure when his second-in-command was having an affair with an actress and all Germany was gossiping about it ?

So he ordered Goering to marry Emmy. Now, Goering is an aristocrat and in his mind making love to an actress and marrying her were two entirely different things. But the Führer was insistent. So Goering, after many bitter protests, had to give way and duly married Emmy. Hitler was present at the ceremony and at the luncheon held afterwards. He gave Goering a magnificent motor-car and Emmy a pair of emerald pendants. And whenever I saw Goering and his wife together it struck me that the Field-Marshal was quite happy in his marriage. She certainly was. Her conceit was tremendous. Her success in having got her Hermann to the altar had obviously gone to her head.

Goering must be extremely wealthy. He always gave lavish presents to his friends and servants. I once found a ring he had lost in his bedroom. He thanked me and a week later I received a small platinum wrist-watch from him.

His personal guards are always getting presents. Sometimes it is only a couple of cigars but often it is a cigarette-case, a radio set, a case of cognac, or a sporting-gun.

He has bought houses for three of his friends, men who served with him when he was in the German Air Force in the last war. A sea-going yacht is another of his presents.

But I don't think he has ever given one to Doctor Joseph Goebbels, the man he hates and despises with a terrifying intensity.

Goebbels is the exact opposite of Goering. He is small, slim, and dark. No one has ever known him to perform one generous action. The best thing about him is his voice. It can be soft or liquid or vibrant with passion. Hitler's is harsh and, at times, inclined to be nasal. Goebbels' is far more attractive. He uses it a lot, for he rarely stops talking.

Once, in the early summer of 1938, he must have spoken a little too much for Goering's patience. They were both staying at Berchtesgaden and towards the end of Goebbels' stay I met him on the stairs. I stood deferentially pressed against the wall as he went past me, but I glanced at his face. It was set in an ugly scowl and a livid weal marked one cheek. Naturally, I was curious and started asking cautious questions from other members of the staff. From one of them I finally got the truth.

Goering had just come from a drive. He was walking through the entrance-hall when Goebbels appeared. Goebbels made some witty but malicious remark about Goering's appearance, a remark which the genial Hermann would probably have laughed aside if it had come from anyone else.

But he did not laugh. He pulled off one of his long, heavy leather gloves and slashed the little doctor across the face with it. Then walked on. A guard on duty saw the whole incident.

Naturally Hitler asked for some explanation of Goebbels' marked face and Goering said what had happened. Hitler was annoyed.

"I can't have this continual squabbling!" he cried. "You behave like children."

Goering scowled and said nothing. He refused to apologize. So did Goebbels. Their hatred of each other was far too bitter for even Hitler to be able to quench it.

Goebbels is a dandy. But, of course, nothing can conceal his deformed foot, a physical infirmity of which he is extremely sensitive. It must account for much of his venom and malice. He always treated the servants at Berchtesgaden with insolence and was continually complaining about their work. Fortunately no one took much notice of these complaints.

I don't believe that Goebbels believes in anything. He was behind every attack on religion that was launched during my stay at Berchtesgaden. And he infected Hitler with the same hatred of Christianity.

In January 1937 Goebbels, who is a good driver, took his car out on the roads east of Berlin. On his way back he passed through the village of Werneuchen without slackening speed. Just as he reached the outskirts an elderly man stepped into the road. Goebbels made no attempt to swerve. He hit the man and sent him flying high in the air. He hit the ground a broken, shattered mass of flesh. Goebbels reached Berlin and then had one of his agents phone the village to find out whom he had killed. It was the village priest.

"And that was the most pleasant afternoon's driving I've ever done," Goebbels always declares when he tells this story. Naturally no details of his exploit were allowed to appear in the German Press. This censorship was hardly necessary, for he told everyone who met him about it. He hates Roman Catholics and was always urging Hitler to take severe steps against them.

But Goebbels is a friend of the Jews. When I say that I do not mean that he does not attack them in the Press he controls. He does, most vehemently. Yet he has several Jewish friends. Hitler's hatred of Jews is something pathological. Goebbels only pretends. I know this because one of his friends is a former Jewish librarian of the Preussische Staatsbibliothek in the Unter den

Linden, and several times this man has been sent out of
Germany to collect rare books for Goebbels' library.
Goebbels is the best educated of all the Nazis and he has
got together a magnificent library of eighteenth-century
literature.   Hitler sometimes borrows books from him—
a thing which Goebbels hates for the Führer always reads
with a large red pencil in his hand and scores scarlet
lines alongside the passages of which he approves.

Goebbels' affairs with women are notorious throughout Germany.   Most of them are conducted in a villa
he owns in the Paulsbornerstrasse in the Charlottenburg
district of Berlin.   I have never seen it, only photographs.
But I have spoken to servants who have worked there.
They all agree on one thing : it is one of the most luxurious houses in Germany.   From there start the periodic
scandals which continually anger the Führer.   I cannot
imagine Hitler worrying over much about the morals of
his leaders, but he certainly worries when the man in
the street begins gossiping.   And the Führer is very fond
of Magda Goebbels, the little doctor's wife.

He once showed it very pointedly.   Hitler invited
Goebbels and his wife to Berchtesgaden for two or three
days.

I saw Goebbels arrive, but out of the car there stepped—
not his wife—but a very attractive blonde with an
exciting figure.   She was a Viennese and a very minor
star, but also the star in Goebbels' life for the moment.
She wore a long sable coat that must have cost thousands
of marks. She entered the house and was taken to a room
adjoining that of Goebbels.   Neither of them saw the
Führer until dinner that evening.   As they entered the
dining-room, Goebbels led her up to where Hitler was
standing and introduced her.   Hitler ignored her.

"Where is Magda ?" he snapped.

"Ah, she asked to be excused," explained Goebbels.
"She said she was feeling too ill to make the journey."

Hitler at once went to his study and got on the phone
to Berlin.   He spoke to Magda, discovered that she was
perfectly fit, and had just been shelved in favour of the

film-star. He gave her a personal and pressing invitation to Berchtesgaden and told her that a military plane would be waiting for her early next morning. That done he went back to where Goebbels was shifting about uneasily and announced that the Viennese would find an excellent meal served in her room in a few minutes.

I served that meal—to a pale-faced and very frightened young woman.

"What have I done?" she cried. "He made me come. I knew there'd be trouble. And now I'm ruined." Actually she was far from being ruined, for she remained Goebbels' mistress for several months and acquired a fortune in jewellery.

She left after breakfast next morning and Magda arrived shortly afterwards to be greeted by an effusive Hitler and a sulky husband.

Hitler knows, however, that Goebbels would be difficult to replace. He is a genius at propaganda. Time and time again when he has been at Berchtesgaden the line has been cleared to Berlin and he has picked up the phone and dictated a two-thousand word article with hardly a pause for breath. The article has appeared next day in every German paper and confirmed the wavering faith of thousands of Hitler's followers. I have good reason to detest the Nazis but I have always tried to be fair to them. And even about Goebbels there is something good to be said. He is morally evil but he has the energy of a demon. He works at tremendous speed and never for a moment lets his finger slip from the pulse of the German nation. Hitler cannot use a dictaphone. But one is never far from Goebbels' side. I have heard him dictating into it far into the night. Nothing is too small to escape his attention. He himself has read every school book to make certain that every fact they contain is a piece of Nazi propaganda. That is why Hitler allows him to go on living and why, in spite of his unpopularity with every other big Nazi, Hitler still listens to him. He is one of the few Nazis entitled to wear the Führer's Chain.

F

This has never been described before. It is a small golden chain of five links. Each one is stamped with a minute swastika and the chain ends in a tiny gold medal on one side of which is the Führer's profile and on the other an eagle with outstretched wings clutching a swastika in its claws.

Only five men possess this chain. They are Goering, Goebbels, Himmler, Hess, and Streicher.

Himmler is particularly proud of his. Presumably he has earned it by his devotion to murder. For he is the mass-murderer of the Third Reich.

We always spoke of 'Heinrich and his little black bag', because whenever he arrived at Berchtesgaden he was never without a black leather brief-case. The case never left his side. When he travelled it was attached to his wrist by a thin steel chain.

His secretary told us that it contained reports on the latest activities of the Gestapo and plans for the future. Certainly he and Hitler spent long hours together going over its contents and when he left a new reign of terror began throughout Germany.

Himmler is slim with thin sandy hair, watery blue eyes, and a receding chin. He neither drinks nor smokes and is a vegetarian. He has two hobbies—keeping rabbits and collecting china. He breeds rabbits at his country home and seems to get a good deal of pleasure out of this mild pastime. His collection of china has been, of course, built up largely by theft. His Gestapo agents have orders to seize any pieces of china they see when they raid a home. They are always sent to Himmler to see if they are valuable and rare enough to go into his collection. Museums, too, have been raided.

Himmler's health is bad. Everyone at Berchtesgaden declares that, although long ago pronounced cured, he still suffers from the effects of venereal disease contracted when he was only a lad of twenty. It is this, they say, that accounts for his bad eyesight. It is terribly bad. The reports he has to read are typed for him on a machine whose letters are three tenths of an inch high.

He never visits ordinary cinemas for the same reason. He is rarely without a headache—for which he was taking drugs when I knew him. His voice is soft and gentle, with a slight lisp. The queerest thing about him is his personal vanity. He is as proud of his looks as a beautiful woman. He has a most elaborate travelling-case which I have unpacked at least twice. It is packed with mysterious highly-scented pomades, after-shaving lotions, a complete set of manicure equipment, and a gadget made of steel and rubber which, when its wire was plugged into an electric power point, vibrated briskly and was then smoothed up and down the face. It was supposed to keep the skin fresh and youthful. And the master of the Gestapo spent half-an-hour each morning trying to beautify his skin with it.

He was extraordinarily superstitious. He believes three to be his lucky number so does everything in threes —a habit which can be very trying to his staff, as, for example, when he insists on three of them being present when he only wants to speak to one of them. That situation has often happened. He always eats three apples at once, must have three potatoes on his plate, and always gives three marks as a tip. He had an ordinary pen which he has used since he was a young man. He refuses to write with any other and must have worn out hundreds of nibs signing the decrees which have brought torture and death to so many German citizens.

In spite of his childish vanity he is interested in no woman but his wife. He has had affairs, but they are only momentary, purely physical affairs. He is really in love with his wife, but she has had no softening influence on him. I only saw her once. A woman of rather faded prettiness, she had an acid tongue and severe narrow lips. I did not see her smile. I doubt if she can. Of course, her clothes are enough to destroy any woman's sense of humour. I imagine she is easily the worst-dressed woman throughout the Reich—which is saying a good deal. She always wears woollen stockings and drab shapeless dresses. Her hair is greasy and her skin blotched and sallow. But her Heinrich obviously finds her to his taste.

Himmler is at least sane although a monster of cold cruelty. But no one could imagine Julius Streicher as anything but a pathological specimen whose home should be the nearest lunatic asylum. Yet Hitler refuses to hear a word against this pot-bellied, bald-headed, bandy-legged pervert. I have often seen him at close quarters. Perhaps the most repulsive thing about him are his lips—full, fleshy and red, they are always moist for he drools as he speaks. His voice is like a parrot's—and his conversation is that of a peculiarly blasphemous cockatoo. He is, of course, editor of the *Stuermer*, a paper packed with anti-Jewish obscenity and, when he begins to speak about the Jews, he shouts louder than his Führer. Flecks of foam fly from his lips, sweat breaks out on his forehead, and his whole body trembles with rage.

He is an epileptic. One evening he made his excuses to Hitler and retired to bed early. I was coming along the corridor past his bedroom when I heard a terrible scream come from his door. Without thinking, I opened it and glanced in. The Jew-baiter was lying on the carpet, his body rigid, his eyes rolled up until I could only see their whites, and a trickle of blood running down his chin where he had bitten his tongue. I at once rang the bell summoning his personal attendants. When they arrived I was hustled out of the room. Next morning they came to me and warned me to say nothing of what I had seen.

"Streicher was tired," they said, "and worry and nervous strain had made him faint. But if you are wise, forget about it."

. He had not fainted. He was in the throes of a fit and I heard later that these fits occur fairly frequently, sometimes as often as once a week.

He is, too, a sadist. In Nuremberg, the city he rules, he often goes to the local jail and flogs a few prisoners until they scream for mercy—then relates the whole story of the flogging, with many details, to Hitler on his next visit to Berchtesgaden.

He has three illegitimate children about whom no one is supposed to know anything. I know the names of two of them—Kurt and Konrad. The third child is a daughter whom I have never seen and whose name I do not know. I was told that she had a responsible post in the Ministry of Propaganda. Kurt is twenty. Konrad seventeen. They are both S.S. men stationed in Breslau. Already Kurt has been involved in a scandal, for in September 1937—I believe, although I am not sure of the exact date—he attempted to rape the daughter of a wealthy Breslau tradesman named Willi Doerr. He spent a night in a cell, but was released the next morning and Doerr was warned to keep his mouth shut. The girl was sent to one of the Labour Camps for women somewhere in the Rhineland.

All the women servants at Berchtesgaden hated Streicher. He leered at them and they were lucky to escape with a pinch or two if he met them on the stairs or in any of the corridors.

His great worry is his baldness. He will listen to any quack who hints that he has a cure. Several times he arrived at Berchtesgaden wearing a contraption called a magnetic wig. It looked rather like a bit of material cut from a hearthrug that had seen better days. It had, of course, no effect but he spent hours gazing into the mirror to see if any hair had begun to sprout.

If it were not for his anti-Jewish mania Streicher would be a negligible figure. Everyone laughs at him behind his back. But he has considerable influence with Hitler, largely because he has an apparently inexhaustible supply of dirty stories which he relates with relish at the slightest provocation. They are one of the few things which amuse the Führer. Perhaps it is in payment for these jokes that Hitler always gives him such magnificent birthday presents. In 1937 he sent him a Mercédès car. In 1938 it was a cinema projector made by the best technicians in Germany together with the complete film of the Olympic Games made by Leni Riefenstahl.

Personally I should prefer the present Hitler gives Rudolph Hess every year—a cheque for £5,000. Hess was imprisoned with Hitler after the abortive Munich *Putsch*. During this imprisonment much of *Mein Kampf* was written and Hess had far more to do with it than most people imagine. Many of the ideas in this 'Bible of the Nazis' come from Hess. Hitler knows this and so every year, out of the enormous royalties he draws from the sale of the book, he gives Hess £5,000. Hess's real name should be Yes. He has never been known to contradict Hitler. His invariable answer is : "Yes, *mein* Führer." He must be too stupefied with drugs to be able to think for himself. I, for one, have never believed the stories that Goering is a drug fiend. But I know that Hess is. He cannot live through a day without a dose of heroin and he has to have an extra large dose every time he makes a speech. Apart from this he is a man with no vices. His only job in life is to do exactly as Hitler orders. He has spent long weeks at Berchtesgaden but actually I hardly remember him. His personality is so colourless that one never noticed his presence.

One could not, though, forget von Papen. Largely because he rarely came except to be abused by Hitler for some stupid blunder. The only reason he is still alive is because Hitler is still a snob at heart and von Papen is an aristocrat and one of the men who first introduced Hitler to fashionable, moneyed society.

Von Papen is a dandy. All his clothes came from London—a city which he admires. He imitates the English. His favourite drink is whisky, of which he manages to drink nearly a bottle a day. But it did not, when I met him at any rate, seem to have impaired his capacity for love-making. This grey-haired, shifty-eyed diplomat imagines he is the Romeo of the Reich. He is a devout Roman Catholic, but his religion is no check on his philandering. But I will say one thing for him—his amours are not of the kitchen. He likes big game and you will find that his current mistress is usually one with a dash of royal blood in her veins. Hitler usually gives them a warm welcome to Berchtesgaden, much warmer, in fact, than he gives von Papen.

For von Papen seems unable to resist putting his foot into things. Everyone knows the major diplomatic blunders he has repeatedly made. Not everyone realizes that what he does in public life he does with even more vigour in private life.

Here are two examples : Dr. Robert Ley, Nazi Labour leader, got very drunk in Cologne in 1929. He produced an axe from somewhere, went into the Ratskeller and chopped merrily away at the frescoes there. Someone took a snap of Ley at work and of Ley being led away by policemen. It made a picture that was very valuable propaganda to anti-Nazis. Von Papen saw it and was so amused that he bought the negative, had a huge print made of it and hung it in his study, giving it pride of place on the walls. It remained there after the Nazis came to power. In fact it was hanging there in all its drunken glory when von Papen gave a small party and among the guests was Dr. Ley himself.

As I shall presently tell, Hitler grew very fond of one Jenny Jugo. And at the same time cast longing eyes on a Bavarian woman named Eva Braun. Fräulein Jugo was staying one week-end at Berchtesgaden and was having tea with Hitler on the Saturday afternoon. Von Papen was announced and invited to join them. For once he was on fairly good terms with the Führer. This truce did not last for long. About ten minutes to be exact. For von Papen informed Hitler that he had been lunching with Eva Braun and that she had asked him to send her love to the Führer—a message which angered Hitler and Fräulein Jugo equally.

A great admirer of von Papen was Miss Unity Mitford. She thought he was 'so distinguished.' Her feeling for Hitler went beyond admiration. She worshipped him. She was a frequent visitor to Berchtesgaden where her favourite occupation was taking snaps of Hitler with a camera he had given her. She was always an honoured guest but we could never discover whether it was because

Hitler was genuinely fond of her or because he saw in her a way to get Nazi propaganda circulating through the ranks of English society.

No foreigner is allowed to wear the swastika badge, but Hitler had a gold one specially designed for Miss Mitford with the swastika on one side and an engraving of his signature on the other.

I often acted as Miss Mitford's personal maid at Berchtesgaden. She had lovely clothes. On her dressing-table a signed photograph of Hitler always stood. She carried it around with her whenever she travelled.

I once ventured to ask her if she was really fond of Germany. Her face lit up.

"It is a marvellous country led by the greatest genius in history," she declared, "and Britain's truest friend is Adolf Hitler. Together the two countries would be invincible. I would sacrifice anything to bring about an alliance between them."

I asked her what she thought of the revolution in Germany's social life since the Nazis came to power.

"It is magnificent," she said, without a moment's hesitation. "All the riff-raff have been imprisoned. Only clean-living men and women are allowed to live peacefully in Germany now. Hitler has been hard to the others. Sometimes I think he has not been hard enough."

Her eyes blazed with fanatical fervour as she said this. She paced up and down her bedroom.

"I hate the little petty-minded critics who attack the Führer. What can they know of what goes on inside his mind? He is a man, a real man, superior to every other. One day everyone in the world will recognize his greatness."

I agreed with her. There was nothing else to do.

I have seen her drinking coffee with the Führer. She is like a woman in a trance when he speaks.

Very different from King Carol of Rumania who came to see Hitler at the Führer's invitation. I liked him tremendously. He behaved like a king who knew exactly how to treat ex-house-painters. Hitler attempted some of the tactics that succeeded with Schuschnigg. Only they did not succeed with King Carol. For when Hitler shouted the King shouted back—in a voice that startled the Führer into temporary silence. And, apart from the delight most of us felt in having someone in the house who could stand up to Hitler, we liked King Carol's generosity. He gave us all a fifty-mark tip when he left.

There were many other visitors. Two or three times a year, for instance, Hitler gave a dinner to selected local Nazi leaders. They were extremely dull affairs, for the guests were over-awed by the presence of their Führer and just sat there hardly daring to touch the food while Hitler harangued them on various points of Nazi policy. At these functions—and also when Hitler gave a party for children—Hoffmann was always present. Hoffmann is an old friend of Hitler's and an extremely wealthy man—wealthy because he owns the copyright in every picture of the Führer. He is a brilliant photographer and attends these dinners so that he can take a picture of Hitler feasting loyal Nazis and circulate them throughout Germany to show how the Führer repays the men who are loyal followers of his teachings. Hoffmann's palatial studios are in Munich—Number 74, Teresienstrasse. When they are not occupied in producing pictures of Hitler patting the heads of little children, they turn out albums of obscene photographs which sell throughout the Balkans. So, what with Hitler and dirt, Herr Hoffmann does very nicely.

I have not mentioned any of Hitler's women guests—but only because they deserve a chapter to themselves. Hitler's relations with women is a fascinating story. Now, for the first time, the world can read the truth about them.

CHAPTER FIVE

H ITLER IS A BACHELOR. DR. GOEBBELS
says he will never marry because he has only one love
in his life—Germany. Hitler may remain single, but to
say that Germany is his only love is nonsense. It may be
good propaganda. But that is the best that can be said
for such a fantastic statement. For Hitler is woman
crazy. He is discreet and his love affairs are not always
the normal affairs of a healthy man. But he cannot exist
without women.

He owes his present position to women. Women
flocked to his meetings long before he was much more than
a soap-box speaker. It was the woman's vote which swept
him to increasing victories at the polls. The wives of the
great Ruhr financiers met him and were fascinated.
Their husbands' money soon afterwards began to flow
into the Nazi till.

That is ancient history, well-known to every student
of the Nazi movement. But what is not well-known at
all is the story of Hitler's personal, intimate friendships
with women.

Let us go back some years. Of this particular story
I can only say that it was told to me on three different
occasions by three different people—one of them a Nazi
of high rank. I cannot vouch for its truth beyond this
and beyond the fact that the girl did exist and did
commit suicide.

Her name was Geli Raubal and she was the daughter
of Hitler's half-sister.

She was nineteen when Hitler first met her in 1921.
He fell head over heels in love with her. She liked him
but her liking never blossomed into love. Adolf,
then only Member Number Seven of the National
Socialist Labour Party, began to neglect his political
work. He failed to turn up at meetings, preferring to

spend his evenings walking in the Munich parks arm in arm with slim, dark-haired Geli. His days were spent in writing passionate letters.

His love was frowned upon by family opinion which disliked the idea of Hitler marrying his step-niece. And, although Geli appreciated the intensity of Hitler's love, was flattered by it and had a real affection for him, she felt she could not marry him.

Yet she dared not tell him the truth. Already she felt what millions of others have since come to know—that Hitler cannot be ignored, cannot have his wishes slighted. Night after night she sat on her bed wondering what to do. She could not tell him that she would never marry him, yet each day she felt she was getting further enmeshed in this rapidly ripening romance. So, in the end, she took what seemed to her to be the only way out.

On the night of December 3rd, 1921, she said goodnight to Hitler at the door of her home. Half-inarticulate with desire Hitler put his arms round her and drew her close to him. He rained passionate kisses down on her upturned mouth, his searching hands caressing her trembling body. Finally she broke away and ran indoors.

In the safety and peace of her own room she sat down to write a letter. It was to Hitler and told him that she could not marry him. She slipped out with it to the post then, when she returned, locked herself in her room and turned on the gas.

She was dead when they found her next morning. And so ended the first romance of Hitler's life. It nearly drove him to suicide. For weeks he paced the streets of Munich, speaking to no one. He ate hardly anything. Great black rings of approaching madness circled his eyes. Politics were forgotten. It seemed that life was at an end for him. Gradually he recovered. The needs of the Party once again called to him. He decided to forget his suffering in work. And, until he came to power, he never loved another woman.

But with the achievement of supreme power, women once again began to stir his senses.

Goebbels soon realized that Hitler had not the indifference to women that his propaganda declared. He decided to make use of this knowledge. If Hitler decided to marry, Goebbels also decided that he would marry a woman which he—Goebbels—had chosen. In this way the little doctor sought to strengthen his position.

Renate Muller was the first victim to be sacrificed to this plan of Goebbels.

Long before I entered Berchtesgaden she had been one of my screen heroines. She was pretty. She could sing and dance and she had a spontaneous gaiety absent from so many German girls. And when she began visiting Berchtesgaden I discovered that her charm was not merely assumed in a film-studio. She was as friendly and gay in real life as she was on the screen.

Goebbels arranged her first meeting with the Führer. He led up to it very cleverly by praising her acting to Hitler and then suggesting that some of her films should be shown in the private cinema. Hitler, who likes film shows, at once agreed. He was entranced by her and ordered Goebbels to invite her to spend a few days at Berchtesgaden.

The invitation was given and accepted. Renate Muller arrived one Friday in time for dinner. The meal passed off without unusual incident. After it was over Hitler offered to show Renate round the house. They set off together, accompanied by Goering, Goebbels and his wife, and one or two other guests. Hitler said little as the procession passed from room to room, pausing in each one. Finally they arrived at the library. Renate asked Hitler some questions about the books there. While he was answering her she noticed out of the corner of her eye, that the others had gone on into a further suite of rooms.

She was alone with Hitler. This is what happened— it would be unbelievable if Renate had not told her friends and I had not heard it myself from one of their maids.

Hitler suddenly stopped speaking about the books. He looked for a few moments at Renate, then stretched out his arm in the Nazi salute. He held it steadily for several minutes, then dropped it to his side.

"I can hold my arm like that for two solid hours," he declared.

Renate was too amazed to answer.

But Hitler went on :

"I never feel tired when my Storm Troopers and soldiers march past me and I stand at the salute. I never move. My arm is as if of granite—rigid and unbending. But Goering can't stand it. He has to drop his hand after half-an-hour of the salute. He's flabby. But I am hard. For two hours I can keep my arm stretched out in the salute. That is four times as long as Goering. That means I am four times stronger than Goering It is an amazing feat. I marvel at my own power."

And with that he turned and walked out of the room.

That was Hitler's first attempt at love-making to Renate Muller. She would still be alive to-day if it had been his last. But as that first week-end wore on he began to pay her more and more attention.

On the last night of her stay he invited her to see herself on the screen in his cinema. No one else was present—except the operator who managed to see a good deal from the projecting box. Hitler ordered Renate's latest film to be shown. They sat side by side to watch it. Half-way through Hitler's hand found Renate's. He said nothing. A few minutes later it slipped to her thigh and began to stroke its smooth contours. Renate let a little smile flicker across her lips. The Führer was not, after all, immune to the attractions of a pretty woman and, of course, Renate was flattered. She did nothing to check his ardour and so, until the film flickered to an end, Hitler indulged in an orgy of petting.

Next morning Renate was flown back to Berlin in Hitler's private plane. At her flat she found great bowls of exotic flowers that Hitler had sent. For several weeks he sent her flowers every day. There were other and more costly presents—diamonds and furs. Goebbels' propaganda machine began to act. Articles appeared throughout the Nazi Press praising Renate Muller as Germany's greatest actress. Cinemas were ordered to show revivals of her earlier films. Her photograph appeared in all the fashionable papers.

Renate acted in the theatre as well as in the film-studios and so she had to stay in Berlin. Hitler left Berchtesgaden and for over two months we never saw him. We all knew why. He just could not stay away from Renate. She visited him at the new resplendent Chancellery. Twice he went to her flat and each time the immediate neighbourhood was ringed round by discreet but heavily-armed Gestapo agents. On the second visit he left at four in the morning. They had been alone since midnight.

Renate saw herself as the wife of Germany's ruler. She did not love him. She liked him and the position he could offer her dazzled her imagination. Goebbels was triumphant. If Renate became Frau Hitler she would remember who had introduced her to the Führer and Goebbels' position would be more than ever secure. And if she had married Hitler the history of the world would have been changed. For she was a kindly girl and would have done everything she could to swing Hitler round from his insane cruelty. But a Jew made it impossible. It is this which has intensified Hitler's hatred of the Jews. I have heard him say that, not content with trying to ruin the economic life of Germany, the Jews had tried to destroy his own personal happiness.

"But they shall pay ! But they shall pay !" he used to scream.

It is true that a Jew made his marriage with Renate Muller impossible. But it was not the Jew's fault. He was the only son of a Jewish millionaire whose family had lived in Germany for the past two hundred years.

The millionaire died two years before Hitler came to

power and his son inherited his fortune. When Hitler became Chancellor this young Jew was not flung into a concentration-camp. His business connections with foreigners were too valuable for that. He had to live quietly but he was not molested He often went for early morning rides in the Tiergarten in Berlin and it was there that he met Renate Muller, riding on a horse given her by Hitler.

Renate disbelieved in anti-Semitism. She thought it pernicious nonsense. It seemed even more wicked and foolish after she had met this particular Jew two or three times. It was not long before she was madly in love with him. But even Renate, crazily in love, realized that this could not be an open romance. So there were secret meetings, long motor-drives into the heart of the country, dinners in country beer-gardens.

But always the shadow of persecution hung over them. Renate felt disaster ahead and she finally persuaded her lover to leave Germany. It was not easy, but with money anything can be accomplished—even in Nazi Germany. The Jew crossed into Czecho-Slovakia—still a free and independent State—and from there made his way to Paris.

Shortly afterwards Renate went to Paris for a holiday. She dare not stay there. She had too many relatives living within the Reich and she knew that if she refused to return they would end in a concentration-camp. But together they spent a glorious month in Paris. Hitler was forgotten. Renate was quite willing to sacrifice her future as the first woman of Germany for a single night of passionate love-making with her Jewish lover. And she had weeks of such nights.

Paris is not a city which encourages caution. The two lovers flung off all restraint. They were seen everywhere together. So it was not to be wondered at that the Gestapo heard of this love-affair. Its agents were then scattered everywhere in the big cities of Europe. And these agents are clever. They see without being seen. Two of them, stationed in Paris, made it their sole job to shadow Renate and her lover. And they shadowed them with cameras.

It was not until the first week of Renate's holiday was over that they got on to the trail. Then, for the next three weeks, they were never far away and, when Renate was ready to return to Germany, they had a complete dossier of her movements, backed up by a series of revealing snapshots of her riding in the Bois with the young Jew, dancing with him, her body pressed close to his, dining with him, drinking with him in the cabaret shows off the Place Pigalle, doing everything that lovers do in public.

This dossier went in the diplomatic bag to Himmler. If it had gone to Goebbels things might have turned out differently. As I have said, he has no real, personal hatred of the Jews and he has a real desire to marry Hitler off to some girl of his own choice. So he would probably have suppressed the dossier. Not Himmler. He hates Goebbels and the Jews too much.

Himmler made a special trip to Berchtesgaden with this incriminating material. He saw Hitler and spread it out on the desk in front of him. Hitler went white with fury as he read the dossier and glanced through the photographs. He gave orders that Renate Muller must be brought to him the moment she crossed the frontier on her return.

I and two S.S. men were sent to Aachen to meet her. I was to act as her maid until and after she arrived. Her own maid was to be sent on to Berlin. Before I left I was given strict warning not to discuss the Führer with Renate and to forget everything that Renate herself might discuss with me

As the train pulled up in the station at Aachen, two Gestapo men took us to Renate's carriage. It was late at night. The train had come from Brussels, where she had spent the last two days of her holiday. The S.S. men were going to burst into the carriage. I stopped them.

"Let me be the first to tell her the Führer wants her,"

I said. "You will only terrify her and the last thing we want is any kind of a scene."

So I told Renate. At first she smiled, thinking that Hitler could not bear to be separated from her a moment longer than was necessary. I did not smile. She saw the look on my face and clutched my sleeve.

"What's the matter? Is anything wrong?" she demanded. I soothed her as best I could, and told her the truth—which was that I knew nothing and that the only thing she could do was to obey the Führer's orders.

The four of us spent that night at Cologne, for we motored on from Aachen in one of the great black saloons that the Gestapo uses. We arrived there at about one in the morning and stayed at the Hotel Mittelhauser in the Marzellenstrasse—a much less expensive hotel than Renate would have chosen for herself. We had two rooms with a door between. I slept in one. Renate slept in the other—but she had to take veronal before she could close her eyes. The two S.S. men dozed in comfortable arm-chairs outside our doors.

After breakfast next morning we set off again. We travelled through the day only stopping for lunch and spent the night at Stuttgart. Next afternoon we reached Berchtesgaden. Renate was worried. She pestered me with questions. None of them I could have answered even if I dared.

She was taken straight to her room on her arrival. She had her dinner there. It was not until eleven-thirty in the evening that she was summoned into Hitler's presence. She asked me stay in her room and wait for her return. As I had no other orders I stayed. It was a weary vigil. She did not return until three in the morning, pale, tired, but no longer frightened.

I made her coffee and she told me everything that had happened.

"The Führer was alone," she said. "He sat at his desk as I walked across the room towards him. I smiled and hoped for the best. For nearly three minutes he never

G

spoke, never even looked at me. Then, with a violence
that overthrew his chair, he sprang to his feet and began
to shout at me.

" 'Whore ! Painted whore, crawling between the sheets
with dirty Jew boys ! That's how you spend your time.
You're wasted on the screen. You should be on the
streets of Berlin. That's your real place. Picking up
men from the gutter.' He screamed the words at me,
his face white, a swollen vein pulsing in his forehead.

"I was frightened. I stepped back a pace or two.
He advanced towards me.

" 'Yes, you've been found out. I know all about
your Paris trip, know how you lived like a cheap and
scented prostitute. But I'm not to be insulted like that.
I am the Führer !'

"He paused and I felt a wild, crazy desire to giggle.
It would have been fatal—fatal quite literally too. I
said nothing.

"He paused for a moment, then rushed over to his
desk, picked up a mass of papers and a bundle of photographs and flung them in my face.

" 'Look at those !' he howled. I knelt and picked them
up. I glanced at a photograph. For a second I saw
nothing. The whole room swam round me. It was a
picture of Herr R . . . walking along the Seine Embank-
ment with his arm in mine. I knew then that everything
had been discovered. I knew too that my life was in
danger. And one thinks quickly then.

"I rose to my feet and looked into the mad staring eyes
of Hitler.

" 'Yes, you are right,' I said.

" He began to shout something, then suddenly stopped
and burst into tears. He cried like a hysterical woman.
It was somehow horrible. His shoulders shook, his lank
hair dripped over his forehead like muddy water, and
tears streamed down his cheeks.

"I felt ashamed that I had to witness the Führer of
the Third Reich at a moment of such humiliation. I
felt sorry for him too.

"Instinctively I knew the right thing to do. I laid my hand softly on his shoulder.

" 'Adolf!' I whispered, 'I'm sorry. I was wicked, criminally wicked, if you like. What happened I don't know. I lost my head. Forgive me. I can only ask for that. I know I do not deserve forgiveness. I ask it as a mercy, not as a right!'

"And, Pauline, it worked. The first mad storm of his rage passed. He sobbed as if his heart was breaking. And then he forgave me. He put his hand in mine, and looked at me.

" 'You were foolish, but I cannot hate you for long,' he said quietly.

"And I knew I had won. Oh, yes, we've been talking ever since. I have had to promise never to see Herr R— again. Which is, of course, a promise I have no intention of keeping."

She laughed, a strained, overwrought laugh. And so the matter was patched up. In spite of what she told me I still don't know how. I can only think that Hitler must have been really in love with her to have swallowed such an insult to his pride. Anyhow, swallow it he did, and for a month or two everything went on as before. He was always in Renate's company.

Then she left Germany again, this time to Monte Carlo. And Herr R— was there. The Gestapo was still active. Once again they discovered the truth, but this time they were slower in swinging into action than they had been in Paris. Renate reached Berlin before they could put the new material they had gathered into the hands of Himmler. What had happened at Monte Carlo one can only guess. It seems as if she said a final good-bye to her lover, and went home prepared to die, for on the night of her arrival back in Berlin she went back to her flat and just before midnight flung herself from her window on to the pavement three storeys below.

An ambulance rushed her to hospital. There were operations, blood transfusions—but they were all no use. She recovered consciousness for only a few moments,

long enough to mutter a few brief, disjointed phrases.
And then she died.

The news was flashed to Hitler. He was at Berchtesgaden and for two days behaved like a madman, screaming hideous threats against the Jews. Renate Muller
had chosen death rather than life-long separation from
the man she loved. Hitler could not see the tragedy of
this. He saw only that a Jew had won a woman whom
he himself desired, and, in his twisted mind, this added
fresh fuel to the leaping flames of his anti-Semitism.

His love for Renate Muller died with her. He soon
had another friend—another film star. This time her
name was Jenny Jugo. She is a small brunette and very
pretty. Her family is poor. They were ordinary Bavarian
peasants a few years ago. But they are good Aryans.

She is another importation of Goebbels. The German
Freedom Station, broadcasting in 1937, suddenly inter-
rupted its illegal programme with this statement : "Frau
Magda Goebbels. Do you want to know where your
husband spends so much of his time ? Well, it's easy to
find out. Ask young Jenny Jugo, for example. She
should know."

The station was right. At that time she was Goebbels'
mistress. When Hitler heard of this he called Goebbels to
account. Goebbels replied by introducing her to the
Führer, and, from that moment, she ceased to be Goebbels'
mistress, becoming Hitler's instead. For all the tales
that say Hitler is impotent are lies. He is not strongly
sexed, and his fondness for women is often only platonic.
But I once heard him say to Goering, "I know what
women are for just as well as you do, Hermann."

He promptly bought Jenny Jugo a villa at Schlangen-
bad, a pretty little village about seven miles from Wies-
baden. She had some sentimental attachment for the
village, although actually it was too far away from either
Berlin or Munich to be convenient. Hitler visited it
three times, twice he only stayed for a night, but on the
third visit he remained from Wednesday to Monday.
And during that time only a handful of people knew

where he was. Jenny Jugo was his mistress for several months. He spent a fortune on her. Let me make a list of the presents I know he gave her, and the money they cost.

1.	A diamond bracelet	....	£7,000
2.	A mink coat	....	£1,200
3.	The Schlangenbad villa	....	£4,000
4.	Two motor-cars	....	£2,000
5.	Three horses	....	£120
6.	A four-seater cabin plane	....	£8,000

A total of £22,320. This huge sum, besides the hundreds of pounds he spent on perfume, flowers, lingerie, and all the other luxuries he showered upon her, is easily the most he has ever spent on a mistress. I doubt if Jenny Jugo loved him. She certainly tantalized him more than any other woman has ever dared to.

She was always late for meals at Berchtesgaden. Once I was walking on a ground floor corridor when I heard a tremendous hammering on a door on the first floor, hammering accompanied by a man's shouts and a woman's screams. I began to run up the stairs to see what it was all about. But Paula Hitler, the Führer's sister, saw me and called me back.

"It is nothing," she said. "Get on with your work." I had to obey her, for she is a very important if unobtrusive person in the Führer's household. Later, I discovered that Hitler had been moody for most of the day, and so Jenny refused to come down to dinner. Hitler had gone to fetch her, only to run up against a locked door. He battered away at it for several minutes, raving and shouting in one of his fits of temper. Jenny had remained adamant, screaming from time to time to add a little more to the noise.

I got used to scenes like this. She insisted on playing practical jokes—jokes which usually ended up noisily Once she gave Goering a rubber sausage. He wrestled with it for a few minutes, then hurled it and the plate on the floor with a crash and a string of resounding oaths. Another time she introduced a parrot into the Führer's aviary. It was quite a normal parrot, except that she had taught it to say : "I'm the Führer ! I'm the Führer !" It caused a lively five minutes when it first spoke in Hitler's hearing. She used, too, to send outrageous wires to Hitler signed with names like Goebbels, Ley, or Goering. Anyone else would have died beneath the headsman's axe.

But not all her amusements were as harmless as these. During her reign at Berchtesgaden Hitler had a room fitted up as a studio with a small stage at one end. On this stage Jenny Jugo used to perform. Her performance was filmed and the film stowed away until Hitler felt in the mood for it to be shown on his private screen. The performance was nearly always the same with very slight variations. It was a strip-tease act. Hitler declared it was art. One Christmas I saw an example of this 'art.' The staff was given a good Christmas dinner, and then a select number of us were taken into the cinema. We saw a long, dreary film about the achievements of the National Socialist régime—which, of course, we applauded heartily, stifling our yawns. The second part of the programme was a short film starring Jenny Jugo.

She entered a luxuriously appointed bedroom. She was wearing a tweed suit—a form of dress of which the Führer strongly approves. She yawned and stretched her arms high above her head, then slowly took off her jacket and dropped it over the back of a chair. Then her skirt dropped to her ankles. The men in the audience sat forward in their chairs. This was getting interesting. Her blouse came off next. Taut stockings were drawn high above her knees, leaving an inch or two of gleaming white flesh before her thighs disappeared into short, skin-tight panties. Her ripe young breasts strained within the confines of an open network brassiere.

With her back to the camera she stooped and took off her shoes and stockings. Her brassiere slipped to the floor, then slowly and with a good deal of seductive pantomime her panties followed. She turned round and faced the camera completely naked.

Then, for ten minutes before getting into bed, she did various exercises. I am sorry I cannot describe them. They threw a terrible light on the perversity of Hitler's sexual desires, and on the mind of the woman willing to enact such obscenities.

Hitler saw this film or one similar nearly every night when she was away from Berchtesgaden. I have never been able to understand why we were allowed to see it, unless it was because the Führer's queer, twisted mind wished to display the charms of the woman he had conquered, and so indirectly boast of his virility.

For at this time the Hitler we had come to know so well was a changed man. We occasionally saw a foreign paper, and I was always amused to read that the Führer was sitting brooding at Berchtesgaden, that he had lost his grip on affairs, that his demoniacal energy was flagging. I knew it was nonsense, a fine example of wishful thinking. Hitler does, it is true, work spasmodically, but I have never known him tired. His periods of inaction have always been due to one thing alone—preoccupation with a woman. Jenny Jugo absorbed all his time and energy during the few months she was his mistress. She was not, though, destined to be a permanent addition to the inmates of Berchtesgaden. She certainly was never near becoming Hitler's wife. Why he abandoned her I never knew. There was nothing tragic about the end of the romance. It just ended. Jenny Jugo took up her normal life in Berlin, and the Führer began to look around for new conquests.

His friendship with Leni Riefenstahl developed, but it never became anything but platonic. He admired her work as an actress and a photographer, and gave her the job of making a complete and so very boring record of the Olympic Games held in Berlin.

With another photographer, however, matters were very different. I have mentioned Hoffmann, the photographer who has made himself a millionaire by taking the Führer's photograph on every conceivable occasion. His chief assistant is a thirty-three-year-old woman named Eva Braun, whose home is in the Wassertorstrasse in Munich.

I made it my business to study this woman very carefully as, for a considerable time, we all thought she was to be the Führer's wife. We were wrong. But, anyhow, here is what she is like.

She is dark, and wears her long brown hair in plaited coils over her ears. She is about five feet four inches tall. Her eyes are brown, her lips full and red, partly hiding slightly prominent teeth. She is plump with a well-developed figure. Her voice is soft, but she has a slight impediment in her speech. It is something between a slight lisp and a stammer. She sometimes sounds as if she is a foreigner speaking German with a slight accent.

She first met Hitler when she went to the Chancellery in Berlin to take some photos of him. They spent a whole afternoon together while he posed in various rooms. At the end of what must have been a very tiring session Hitler declared he had never met such a patient, sympathetic photographer.

He demanded next that she should come to Berchtesgaden and make a further series of photographic studies. She arrived the following week and took countless pictures of the Führer patting children's heads, stroking dogs, sitting at his desk, walking along country lanes, and chatting with the neighbouring peasants—all excellent pieces of pictorial propaganda. When she returned to Munich she went in Hitler's own car, and accompanied by three of his bodyguards.

Photography is her work, but she has a hobby—the manufacture and blending of perfumes. It was Eva Braun who first interested the Führer in perfume. The move was a clever one. She told him about it, and got him so interested that he finally paid a visit to her private laboratory in her Munich home. There she distils and blends her exotic scents. She says that every individual—both man and woman—should wear the scent that suits their character, and so, for her friends, she prepares little flagons of perfume that are supposed to reflect their personality. Hitler has always had a weakness for this kind of quackery, so when she gave him one of these flagons and told him she had been working for two years preparing it, he was flattered and delighted. We at Berchtesgaden were not so pleased, for during the whole of the period of their intimacy the Führer's rooms reeked of this particularly cloying scent.

Their friendship developed rapidly. Goebbels was angry. Here was a woman about whom he hardly knew anything—yet she was well on the way towards being Hitler's mistress. His vicious, malevolent mind began scheming and plotting. But his chance to strike did not come immediately. Not for nearly two months, when Eva Braun went to a fashionable party in Berlin. Goebbels was invited. He arrived late and, as he was announced, stood in the doorway and let his beady ferret-eyes rove round the room. Suddenly he drew himself up.

"I cannot stay here," he said in a cold voice. "I recognise someone in this room who is of partly Jewish blood."

He stared directly at Eva Braun, turned, and left the room and the party. Needless to say, the party was not an immense success. Next morning the story was repeated all over Berlin with a good deal of embellishment. Eva Braun was branded as a full-blooded Jewess. Hitler heard of this, and at once ordered an investigation into her ancestry. It was proved that she was a pure Aryan. Hitler was furious at Goebbels' insult. He made him send a letter of apology to Fräulein Braun and publish a series of laudatory articles throughout the German Press, extolling her artistry with a camera. Hoffmann, too, felt he had to take his revenge on the little doctor. For all I know he may be still taking it, for it consisted of having camera candid shots taken of Goebbels, each one emphasizing the club-foot from which Goebbels has the misfortune to suffer. They are not published in

Germany, but they are circulated privately, and cause Goebbels considerable distress.

This little business seemed to confirm the Führer in his admiration for Fräulein Braun. At any rate, immediately after the question of the lady's descent was satisfactorily settled, they went off together on a 'honeymoon'—to Goering's country mansion, Karin Hall, not far from Berlin. Goering, who usually did not approve his master's interest in women, this time gave his whole-hearted co-operation to the affair. He saw in it a way of annoying Goebbels.

When they came back to Berchtesgaden I saw a good deal of her. I did not like her. She seemed to have a large streak of cruelty in her character. Her own maid came with her, and she often came down to the servants' quarters with her eyes red from weeping, and sometimes a deep red stain disfigured her face where her mistress had slapped it. In revenge she had collected a fund of malicious stories about her. One she told us I think is too good to be kept to myself.

It was on one of Eva's visits to the Berlin Chancellery to keep a lunch appointment with the Führer. She entered through the private door which leads into a great hall with highly polished parquet flooring. This hall ends in a large door leading to Hitler's private apartments. On either side of the door, facing it, stand two burly bodyguards in immaculate uniform. They stand rigidly at attention for three-hour shifts, and are more like statues than men.

Eva, proud at having lunch with Germany's supreme ruler, walked across the hall, head held high. A little too high, for, just as she was approaching the open door flanked by the bodyguards, her heel slipped on the polished floor. She flung her hands out to save herself, and managed to grab the trouser-seat of the right-hand guard. For a second he remained motionless, but as Eva's feet slid from under her and her clutch on him tightened they both crashed to the floor together. A second later Hitler appeared in the doorway just in time to see the flurry of Eva's legs as she struggled to scramble to her feet with her skirt almost up to her hips, while the guard found himself with his nose buried in her neck.

Eva Braun is still a friend of Hitler. At least, she was when I left. But their affection had by then reverted to the platonic. But she still saw him regularly, only their conversation ran on politics rather than on love. She hates Britain. I have often heard her jeer at Britain's cowardice. Hitler listened to her with some amusement, but often contradicted her.

"The British are fools but not cowards. They only seem like cowards because they are so badly led. But when they get in the trenches they fight like madmen. I know. I have fought against them," he once declared.

"There are only three countries which produce great soldiers—Germany, France, and Britain. Other countries only play at fighting. Look at the Italians. The only order they understand is the order to retreat. And to-day Germany's soldiers are the best in the world—because they are fighting for ideals, the tremendous ideals of National Socialism !"

Ribbentrop was always friendly with Eva Braun, largely because of this anti-British attitude of hers. I saw very little of the ex-champagne merchant, because when he was at Berchtesgaden he seemed to spend nearly all his time with Hitler and hardly spoke to anyone else. Except Eva. He egged her on to sneer at Britain before Hitler. I once heard him shout : "Englishmen are only savages. They are cunning, but know nothing of culture, nothing of the Germanic way of life. They must be beaten to their knees." And Eva applauded every sentiment like this. Between them they must have done much to inflame Hitler's mind against Britain.

Hitler had another woman friend when I was at Berchtesgaden I cannot say anything about. To me she will always be Fräulein X because it is to her that I owe my freedom. All I can say is that she was the best influence Hitler has ever known. It is a thousand pities for the world that she did not become his wife.

Fräulein Kirstner is another woman who has played and, for all I know, still does play, a tremendous part in Hitler's life. She is forty, plain, comfortably stout, and with no pretensions to any kind of dazzling charm. To me she will always be the greatest mystery in the Führer's life. She was at Berchtesgaden when I arrived. She was there when I left.

She has nothing to do with the running of the establishment. She usually takes her meals in the two rooms in which she lives. But she is a permanency at Berchtesgaden. She does what she likes, goes where she likes, says what she likes—unquestioned. I know she often spends several hours alone with Hitler. And that is about all I do know.

But when the history of Hitler's years of power is fully told I am as certain as I am certain of anything that the world will learn more of Fräulein Kirstner.

She is the mystery woman of Germany. I am convinced that her influence over Germany's destiny has been enormous. Do not ask me why. I can only say that we all thought that, and I am sure our belief will one day be justified.

There are two more things I must say about Hitler and women.

An Austrian psychologist who happened to be a good Nazi and yet a good doctor visited Berchtesgaden. He could not help studying the Führer as a patient. I know what his verdict was, for he told a Munich doctor who afterwards attended me. These were his words. "The Führer is a great man, but that is not to say that he is sane. I admire his work for Germany, but I still have my beliefs as a doctor. If I were speaking of him as a patient I should say he was an ego-maniac with a split personality. One side of him is brutal. The other is weak and sentimental. When this side predominates he needs the company of women. They flatter his ego, reassure him about his virility, and bolster up his pride. That, I am certain, is the only reason why the Führer has affairs with women—not because he is really in love with them, but because he is so madly in love with himself."

And here, more in the nature of a footnote than anything else, because I cannot vouch for it personally, is a story I was told by one of the staff.

It concerns a beautiful Hungarian woman who came to Berchtesgaden and conquered Hitler. The story goes that after he had known her for a week he asked her to be his wife. She smiled and said : "I am afraid it is not so easy to conquer a woman as a country."

She was a Hungarian, so Hitler could do little but smile, even though her words had a bitterness not to his liking.

One reason I was glad to leave Berchtesgaden was to escape from the feverish morbidity of its atmosphere—largely caused by these strange love-affairs. They cast over it the atmosphere of the expensive brothel. There was nothing clean and natural about it. A fog of unclean sex hung over it all.

Chapter Six

I HAVE TOLD SOMETHING OF THE ATMOSPHERE at Berchtesgaden when Schuschnigg was brow-beaten into surrendering his country to the Nazi wolves. But the most dramatic and exciting moments of my life were those at the Berghof on the eve of the actual invasion of Austria.

Himmler, Goering, Goebbels, von Reichenau, and dozens of other military and air force bigwigs were there. Everyone was seized with excitement. Even over the domestic quarters the same tension prevailed. We were warned by Schlieben to be extremely careful in our behaviour and see that not the tiniest detail went wrong when we were serving food or doing our other work.

Hitler had not been to bed for two days. He ate little, too. All the usual schedule was thrown out of gear. He lived on literally nothing but cups of coffee, and he was dictating and interviewing officials without a break.

Those of us who went into his study also noticed that he was working himself up into one of his best states of frenzy. It sounded bad for somebody.

First to catch it was General von Sperrle, the air force chief. I do not know what went wrong, but he was being half thrown out of the study by a Führer screaming with passion as I happened to be passing.

Then everybody began to get into trouble. Even Goering was not immune. Hitler had rows, violent rows, with every important member of his entourage that day.

It seemed that there was general opposition to his plans for the invasion. In fact, the 'rebels' were very angry with him. They held a sort of indignation meeting in the library, and at one time we all thought there was going to be a real revolt. However, the Führer had his own way as usual, and, by the afternoon, things seemed to have quietened down, though of course there was tremendous activity.

Hitler locked himself in his study at three o'clock, and refused to see anyone, although all kinds of urgent business was waiting and all kinds of very important officers were waiting with it.

At four o'clock he rang to the kitchen for coffee. I was told to take it. And I approached the room a little nervously. I knocked and nearly dropped the tray when Hitler's harsh voice howled, "Get away from here!" Then "Who the devil is it?"

I replied, "Coffee, *mein* Führer," in a feeble voice, and there was a grunt. He came and opened the door. As I put the tray on his desk he was talking to himself. "Fools. Sperrle will have to go. I am sick of his superior stupidity. Am I never to get any peace in this house to do my work?"

His voice dropped to a mumbling. I could not distinguish what he was saying. I was glad to get out quickly, for on the Führer's pallid face was a look which told of an imminent fit of hysteria. His eyes were blazing. His face was twitching. I am sure that he did not even notice I was in the room.

I was off duty at six o'clock on that February evening, and I went down to the recreation room to see who was there. I found Greta there playing some card game by herself, and we fell to talking about the day's events. She told me that she had seen Goering threaten to use his dog-whip on ·Himmler, with whom he had been having a tremendous argument.

I said I wished he had done, and as we were laughing the door burst open, and Franz the valet shot in quivering with excitement. "The-the-the Führer's *missing!*" he stuttered. He was almost in a state of collapse with excitement.

Gradually we managed to get a coherent story out of him.

It seemed that von Reichenau, having some matter of the greatest importance to discuss, had marched to the Führer's study and had determined to get in. He knocked but could get no answer. Then he tried the door handle and found that the door was not locked, to his surprise. As he swung it open he saw the Führer's desk empty.

Not that this excited any wonder. The General simply went away, and asked several of the secretaries where the Führer was. No one seemed to know. Gradually everyone who might be expected to know where Hitler was had been asked without result. Then the servants were called. No one had seen him. Every room was visited. Officials went into the garden. Guards were questioned. Still no answer. The Gestapo took charge.

As Franz was talking a Gestapo man came into the room and began to question Greta and me.

By eight o'clock a real toothcomb search had begun. It produced nothing. Panic set in. Even Himmler lost his head a little. He began to threaten his men and to blame them for the Führer's disappearance.

A cordon was put round Berchtesgaden with a circumference of more than four miles. It began to close systematically. A standstill order was given for all traffic in the vicinity. Every stranger for miles was arrested and brought to Himmler.

Some of these unfortunates went through a vicious third degree. All were locked up when the questioning was finished.

Everyone believed that Hitler had been assassinated. I have never seen the Gestapo machine put out of gear so badly.

Then it was suddenly discovered that one of the Storm Troopers was missing. Pandemonium. He was a spy. He had killed the Führer and escaped. He was a foreign agent. He was an Austrian. There was no end to the stories that flashed from lip to lip.

At half-past ten when we servants were in the kitchen, there was a tremendous commotion and we heard cheers. We rushed out. The Führer was entering the house surrounded by excited officials. Himmler came dashing up from his office. The Führer marched to his study and soon all his lieutenants were closeted with him. It was an hour before we heard what had happened.

Hitler had decided to go for one of his solitary walks to think things out. He had left the grounds by a barely-used path to the woods, and had apparently got well up into the mountains before the search began, and was beyond the cordon when it was put into operation.

But the drama was not over. It was to end in tragedy. And the victim was the missing Storm Trooper.

Rudolf Schroder was nineteen and in love with the daughter of a local farmer. He was on guard duty in the grounds on this night, and his post was a box from which he could have seen the Führer pass on his way to the mountains had he been there. He was in the woods with his love, unluckily for him. And the loving couple had found a spot so secluded that they had even escaped detection in the hunt for the Führer.

Unaware of the tremendous events which had taken place, Rudolf blithely returned to the Gestapo quarters at midnight when his duty had ended.

He was sent to Hitler's study, where the panjandrums were still in session.

And before the assembly of the greatest men in Germany, in the presence of the Führer himself, Rudolf Schroder took his own life.

We never got the exact details. But we gathered that the youth, overcome by terror or remorse, had slashed open his throat with a safety-razor blade he had managed to secrete on himself. We got our information of the facts from a guard who was in the room, though for some reason he was very secretive about the whole affair.

We were not in bed until 2 a.m. on that fateful day. Few of us could sleep.

Next day, peace descended. The generals departed. The storm centre had shifted. At noon the rape of Austria had begun.

We did not see Hitler that day. He went away in his big Mercédès very early.

Some say that, in disguise as a common soldier, he had insisted in being the first German to cross the Austrian frontier at the head of the troops. I can well believe that story, for Austria was the Führer's greatest obsession.

He used to spend hours at his telescope looking across the frontier.   Of all his acts of violence to powerless neighbours, I believe that the act against Austria was prompted by real idealism and not by sheer gangster acquisitiveness and lust of power.   I became friendly at this time with Frederick Einzig, one of the Führer's secretaries, and one day he gave me a piece of information which I do not believe has ever been hinted at in the world before.

Hitler and Hess have written a sequel to their famous book, *My Struggle*.   It will never be published until the Führer has achieved the world domination, or a substantial part of it, which is his dream.

As yet the work has no title, but it will be given one on the lines of *How I Did It*.   If it were published now the repercussions might be fatal to the régime, for it is far more frank than the most notorious parts of *My Struggle*.

Moreover, it deals with many famous personalities. Chamberlain is referred to as 'the man who gave me the British Empire because I shouted at him.'

Mussolini is described as "the half-blackamoor ruler of a nation of mongrels."   Hitler's contempt for the Italians and his plans to make them a slave-nation of workers for the Germans are fully described.

Moreover, the book admits openly the tricks and ruses, the bluffings and the impossibility of carrying out threats that the Führer used to get what he wanted from distinguished statesmen.   Astounding secrets of contacts made with pro-Nazi diplomats, politicians, and newspaper proprietors in Britain and the United States, and especially France, are revealed.   There are also full details of how agents secured dossiers of anti-Nazi elements whose names are in Himmler's files.   Many of them are world-famous.

The book is still largely incomplete.   Certain sections are blank, waiting to be filled with actual details, but the whole work is based on the assumption that Britain,

France, Italy, Spain, Portugal, the Netherlands, and Scandinavia are in Nazi hands or at least controlled by puppet governments taking orders from Berlin.

The British Empire and the French Empire, are, of course, fully under the control of Germans.

Names which would astonish the world, I was told, are mentioned as gauleiters in the conquered territories. Einzig would not tell me these, but he said that certain famous men in the democracies, secretly in Hitler's pocket, would be arrested to-day if their Governments would take a glimpse at the new book.

Some hurried changes must have been made in the work, however, since the outbreak of war, because the Soviet problem has not worked out according to plan.

Einzig told me that Russia would be the first Great Power on whom Germany would declare war in order to seize raw materials from the Ukraine in readiness for the attack on the democracies. The book apparently describes how Hitler's 'Fifth Column' in Paris and London ensured that no interference would be forthcoming while the Russians were dealt with.

But the very fact that the book describes events that have not yet occurred is proof of Hitler's faith in his infallibility and in his certainty of the exact fulfilment of his plans.

This book also sets down for the first time many details of Hitler's personal life which have never before been officially revealed. His relations with women, for example, are described in detail. So are many aspects of the private lives of his lieutenants.

One section that would unnerve certain highly-placed Nazis tells why and how they were got rid of at later stages of the game. Those men are even to-day occupying the highest posts in the Party, unaware that they are on the Führer's black list. Not even the Gestapo heads know the contents of *How I Did It.* They would give their right arms for a glimpse. But only Himmler, Hess, and Einzig know that it has been written.

The manuscript is kept in a steel box which is locked

in Hitler's private bomb-proof, fire-proof safe. This is made of an alloy which defies even oxy-acetylene cutting plant, and it has a combination known only to Hess and Hitler. If anyone tried to open it a single mistake in forming the combination would destroy the contents of the safe.

As I mentioned in a previous chapter, I had always at the back of my mind the idea of escape—not simply from Berchtesgaden, but from Germany.

Although I had a pleasant enough life, my existence in the Berghof was so unreal that I could not bear the thought of going on for years and years.

I longed to see my husband again, and to live a normal life in which Hitler and politics were never mentioned. I would not have minded the extremest poverty.

I got my chance through a friend of the Führer himself, who, for obvious reasons, I will refer to here as Fräulein X. She is a woman I have already mentioned in this book. She holds a very high place in the Führer's esteem and is absolutely trusted by him. I was helping her pack clothes one day when she was leaving the Berghof one week-end, and she began to talk to me quite confidentially as women will to domestic servants sometimes. I liked her, and I told her a good deal of my story, ending with my desire to get away.

She seemed to be sorry for me, and said she would try to help. Then she went away and did not come back for a few weeks.

I had almost forgotten our talk when she summoned me to her room and said: "I think I can arrange to get you out of here, Pauline. I can do nothing after that, and you must find your own way out of the country. You must also swear never to reveal how I have helped you."

She need not have asked that. I would never tell a living soul her name, and the facts I am recording here I know will not enable the Gestapo to identify her when they see this book, as they surely will. (I know that a copy will be in your dossier, Herr Himmler!) Now by an amazing coincidence at this time I learned after one of my regular inquiries to the Gestapo that my husband had been released from the Oranienberg concentration-camp and had returned to Karlsruhe. Fräulein X had told me of her plan to let me escape, and I went to her with the new exciting development and she promised to get a message to my husband because I was not, of course, allowed to get in touch with him.

She apparently failed to trace him, however, as I discovered later. Her own scheme to help me was the simplest in the world.

I have told you how Herr Hitler abominated sickness in his house. I was to become an incurable invalid—and a dangerous one, at that !

Fräulein X had a doctor friend, and she brought to the Berghof one day a small bottle of harmless-looking pills.

"These are going to make you very uncomfortable, Pauline," she said. "Take two when you go to bed to-night, and take two more every four hours for the next few days.

"To-morrow morning you will be unable to get up, and you must report sick. The doctors will do the rest, and you will find yourself out of Berchtesgaden before many weeks—for good."

I do not know to this day what those pills contained or what strange disease they produced—or, rather, symptoms. Fräulein X did give me a name, but it was an unfamiliar medical term I had never heard of, and I cannot remember it.

I do know that the pills produced the most alarming results. Next morning my temperature had rocketed, and I had a fever. I did not get up, and when a maid came from the kitchen to see what was the matter I duly reported sick.

About noon, Doctor Tiener, who was in charge of staff medical arrangements, came to see me. He seemed puzzled, and made a very thorough examination.

He ordered me to stay in bed, and banned all food.

I was to have nothing but hot milk. Next day, he came again. Startling things had happened in the night. My skin had gone a peculiar yellow colour, and was very dry to the point of flaking off in places. The doctor was obviously as surprised as I at this development. He stayed only a few minutes.

I was rather alarmed myself, and I began to have doubts about the whole scheme. I was half afraid to go on taking the tablets, but I knew it was now or never so I obeyed instructions and hoped. That evening, Tiener came to see me again, and brought with him a specialist who had arrived to examine one of Hitler's entourage.

The great man gave me another examination and then began to hold whispered consultation with Tiener in a corner. He asked me a number of questions. One was : "Have you ever had gastritis ?" I replied that I had not.

Another was : "Have you ever had jaundice ?" Again I said "No." The specialist took a sample of my blood.

I was left alone for two more days. Then Tiener came again and said I had to go to the sick ward—and was to be isolated. I was alarmed, and asked him what was the matter with me. He was soothing, but vague. "Nothing much, Fräulein. We are simply taking pre-cautions. We shall have you better in no time." He told me that my blood-test had revealed certain symptoms, and that the specialist had prescribed treatment.

I felt weak and feverish still, but apart from the unpleasant skin trouble I had no discomfort.

I went on taking the pills until they were exhausted. I then put the bottle which was plain in a drawer in my dressing-table. I was removed to the sick ward, a per-fectly equipped miniature hospital which is maintained solely for the staff at the Berghof. I was carefully isolated and remained there for some days before the specialist came to see me again.

I was given a pleasant-tasting medicine to take three times a day, and my diet was improved. I was allowed soup, a little fish and dry toast. Milk was the only drink still. I managed to get an inkling of the verdict on my case from the nurse who was put in charge of me. She did not know what was the matter with me, she said, but from scraps of talk between the doctors she had gathered that I had contracted an unusual disease which was infectious, and which was liable to make me a carrier months after I had recovered myself.

I wondered at the ingenuity of Fräulein X's doctor friend. I will never know who he was, but he has my eternal gratitude. I was not so thankful at the time, because shortly after I was put in the isolation ward I began to feel really ill. Also, the skin trouble got worse, and tiny boils began to break out all over my body. I was in agony for two weeks until these yielded to constant dressing.

I was horrified to see myself in a mirror, and I began to wonder if my complexion was going to be ruined for life. Or whether I should always carry disfiguring marks like the victims of smallpox (which my own condition reminded me of rather frighteningly).

However, the fever began to pass, and I felt much better, but my skin remained in an appalling state, and was constantly peeling off.

I was quite happy, however, because I knew that my plans had worked perfectly.

More than a monotonous diet, some physical discomfort, and a rather boring existence without company, would have been needed to upset me seriously.

I was in the sick ward for eight weeks. I was well treated and well looked after. Professor Knoll himself came to see me from time to time.

Often I noticed that he held conferences in the corner of my room with the regular doctor. They nodded agreement many times. One day when I was supposed to have nearly recovered, I was allowed to get up and I was removed from the ward to my own room. Here I was confined for several days, though I did not remain in bed. Schlieben came to see me on the fourth day.

I noticed with amusement that he seemed afraid to approach me too closely.

He said : "We are going to move you from Berchtesgaden, Fräulein. The doctors have told me that you need a long rest before you are fit for work again. You are going to Munich, where you will be able to attend a good hospital regularly for treatment. We shall see that you have enough money and we will provide you with a flat of your own."

I was bubbling with excitement at the success of my friend's plan, but I tried to look pained, and replied :

"I shall be very sorry to leave, Herr Schlieben. Do you think it will be long before I can return ?"

"No, no," he said soothingly. "Just a few months, Fräulein. The rest will do you good."

He well knew that I should never be allowed to work at the Berghof again. What he did not know was that this was my greatest desire. I wondered how the Gestapo would deal with my unusual case. I soon discovered.

On August 19th, 1938, I left Hitler's home in a Gestapo car with my few belongings, which had been carefully searched (though I smuggled out half a dozen things I wanted as souvenirs) in a small suitcase. I was not subjected to more than formal searching because of my good record and the complete success of my illness. A high Gestapo official accompanied me, and when we reached Munich he accompanied me to a small but excellently-furnished flat on the Sendlingerstrasse.

I was pleasantly surprised to find the arrangements that had been made for me. It was a tribute to the esteem in which I was held at the Berghof. It was also a tribute to the efficiency of the Gestapo once more. They wanted me where they could keep an eye on me.

Scharnhaurer, the official who accompanied me, took me into the living-room after we had looked round the flat, for which I had expressed my gratitude, and gave me the warning I had been expecting.

"While you are here, Fräulein, you must be careful with whom you make friends. Remember your actions, even the smallest, will be reported to us. You must tell no one that you served at the Führer's home. You must never gossip, even though you consider it harmless, about anything you know as a result of your work here.

"Your salary will continue to be paid for the time being through the Gestapo offices at Munich police head-quarters, where you will report every month.

"A doctor has been told to call on you, and he will arrange your hospital treatment.

"Remember what I have told you. Good-bye, Fräu-lein."

I made myself comfortable in my new home. I knew that I should have to wait many months before I dare consider the next part of my plan. I was taking no chances until the inevitable police watch on me had been relaxed by good behaviour.

One of the Munich police doctors was detailed to attend me, but he made nothing more than a formality of it, and was very vague when I mentioned innocently that I ought to be attending a hospital. I never went to one, and I knew that the good doctor had been told that my case was hopeless. He had obviously been told to humour me by occasional examinations.

I was very amused to recall my first experience of Munich police headquarters and police doctors at my second visit and later ones. I was now treated with great deference, and I do not believe that anyone knew I had been a prisoner. I did not remind them of it. Anyway, most of the men I remembered had gone away to other duties or, perhaps, to concentration-camps themselves.

For two months I thoroughly enjoyed my new freedom. I was very affluent, because I had my savings as well as my salary and the rent of the flat found for me was only twenty marks a week. I spent my time shopping, going to theatres and cafés, reading, sewing, and a dozen other pleasant little ways. I bought a small spaniel for company, and called him Otto, after Schlieben. I met a number of people, and became friendly with one or two. But I never broke the rule of secrecy laid down by the Gestapo. I always had the feeling that their eye was on me. Mostly it probably wasn't, but that is a very common feeling in Germany.

I was amazed to find a great deal of discontent in Munich among ordinary people. One of the chief complaints was food. Butter and fats were almost impossible to obtain. Clothes were of the very poorest quality. *Ersatz* is a word every German has learned to hate.

But the Germans are born grumblers, and I found no signs of organized protest. The régime was sitting firmly in the saddle. I did not like the food myself. Berchtesgaden had spoiled me, but my freedom was so important to me that I could have lived on air for months.

Gradually I began to get bored, and I knew that soon I must carry my plans a stage further. I had no real idea how I was going to get out of the country. I devised and rejected a dozen plans.

Incidentally, I was always waiting to hear from my husband, for I was still not allowed to get into touch with him by order of the Gestapo. I supposed that Fräulein X had failed to contact him as she promised, and that he had given me up for lost. I remembered that a sister of my mother lived at Breslau, which is not far from the Polish frontier (that used to be).

I thought if I could get there I might find some way of getting into Poland.

I acted with the utmost discretion. First I complained of my inactivity at the Munich police headquarters, and asked them to make a request that I should be allowed to return to the Berghof, as I felt completely well again, and was anxious to get back to work. Of course my application was refused.

I pretended to be very crestfallen when I heard the news, and the Gestapo officials were quite human in their sympathy with me. I waited a week and then wrote to my aunt, carefully omitting any reference to my work at Berchtesgaden, and said I was in Munich alone, and wished to visit her for a little holiday. I told her I had been ill.

She replied with a cordial invitation to stay with her for a few weeks, and I promptly went back to the Gestapo again and showed them her letter and mine.

I begged to be allowed to go, promising that the change would make me really well, and that I should then be able to return to work. I waited three days for a reply, as the request had to go to Berchtesgaden. There was another reason, I suspect. My aunt was being checked up.

In the end I was told I could go, but I was again warned not to break my undertaking about secrecy.

I set off joyfully, and was met by my aunt at the station. She was very pleased to see me, and we asked each other almost simultaneously about my mother. She was heartbroken when I told her what had happened, but she told me not to mention the subject to my uncle when we got home. I soon found out why. My uncle Karl, whom I had never met before, was a good Nazi. He held a high office in the local Party. By profession, however, he was an engineer, and had a very good job with a firm which made machinery for oil-drilling and refining.

This fact was to prove a godsend to me, though I did not know it at the time. My uncle's political character also doubtless caused the Gestapo so promptly to accede to my request for a holiday.

I resolved not to take my Aunt Marthe into my confidence for two reasons. It meant, one, that I should be observing the Gestapo rule and would be taking no chances, and that, two, I should not be incriminating her if I escaped. I did not want to be responsible for sending the poor soul to a concentration-camp.

For many weeks I played the part of nothing more than a niece on holiday, and I pleased my uncle by behaving as a good Nazi and showing my loyalty to the régime on every possible occasion—to the surprise of my aunt, I sometimes felt.

I still had to report to police headquarters for my salary, but this had now been halved, and I was told that I must not mention my 'pension's' source to my relatives.

I told both of them that I had been working as a domestic servant for a high police official in Munich and that I had saved a little money. They asked me nothing for my keep, so it was not necessary to display my 'wealth.'

I did not mention the fact that I had been married.

Whenever I could sneak away I used to make trips by motor-coach to spots near the Polish frontier ostensibly as a sightseer. I reconnoitred the ground thoroughly and, after nearly three months (for the original invitation of a few weeks had been forgotten), I had decided to make a break at a small village called Gorz, little more than a hamlet, and right on the border. It was in a well-wooded area, and frontier precautions seemed to be suitably lax.

But my plans were suddenly changed. My uncle came home one day and announced that he was to go abroad on a big job that would last for many months. This was to accompany and supervise the erection of machinery which was being sent to Rumania to the oil-wells there.

Of course, Aunt was to go with him. But there was the problem of me. I cunningly suggested that I should be left to look after the house for them. They would not hear of it. I must go with them as a real holiday. I had never travelled abroad, and it would be a fine thing for me.

I accepted gratefully, but I wondered how the Gestapo would react to the idea. It seemed hopeless, but I felt that luck was with me, and I boldly went to the police headquarters, and put the facts before them. I pointed out that my uncle did not know that I should have to have their permission, and that he could not be told without learning a number of things he was not supposed to know about me.

The matter was referred to Munich, and then to Berchtesgaden. I waited for a week in suspense. My luck was in. I got permission to accompany my uncle. His position in the Party and my good character had pulled me through.

I could have jumped for joy.

I left Germany on February 12th, 1939—for ever. We went first to Ploesti, in Rumania, where my uncle had to make arrangements for his work, and then we went on to Bucharest for a short stay before a house was found for us near the oilfields. We stopped at a small hotel in the Calea Victoriei, and spent the next few days sightseeing. My uncle was always telling us that this fine city would soon be German. I sincerely hoped not.

I wondered for days how to make my break for freedom, and one day when I had gone out alone I went into a little café for chocolate and began talking to a young man who was obviously a Jew and a German. He told me he was a refugee and that he was being looked after by an underground organization until he could be got out of the country to Switzerland or France. I felt that I could trust him, so I told him of my own case and asked him what he thought it best to do.

We both knew that if I vanished there would be a hue and cry, and that the police would probably find me and hand me over to my uncle. And, though I was in a foreign land, I knew that if the Gestapo really suspected that I was trying to escape their control, they would find their own way of getting me back to Germany, especially in this semi-Fascist country, where German supporters were so strong. The young man, whose name was Vogelbaum, promised to refer the case to his protectors, and to let me know in a few days' time whether they could help me.

I met him again, and he informed me that I could place myself in the hands of his friends if I wished, and that they would hide me until the hunt had died down.

I went back to the hotel, waited for my aunt to go

out, packed a few things in a small case, and returned to the little café and my friend.

I cannot give details of the people who gave me such invaluable help at this time. Nor am I going to describe their organization or the addresses from which they operated. They are doing wonderful work underground, and they are still helping people to-day as they helped me. And although the whole organization is almost exclusively Jewish it does not hesitate to hold out a hand to any Aryan who may be fleeing from the net of the dreaded Gestapo.

It can do no harm to reveal, however, that I was taken into the household of an ordinary Jewish family as a domestic servant. I never left that house for weeks.

I soon saw my name in the newspapers as missing. There were interviews with my aunt and uncle, who were obviously very worried, and, most sinister of all, a big reward was offered by the German Consul-General for my discovery.

A picture and full description accompanied the appeals.

I realized how little hope of success I had on my own, and I thanked God for the protection I had found.

But this amazing organization did more for me. It managed, incredibly, to get me in touch with my husband.

All refugee organizations in Central Europe have a 'secret service' which can match the Gestapo itself for efficiency, and when I told my friends that I wanted to get in touch with my husband, they set the machinery going so efficiently that within a month they had contacted my husband and let him know my whereabouts. They helped him finally to reach Switzerland from Karlsruhe by means which again I cannot reveal. And from there he came to Bucharest.

I shall never forget that day of reunion.

I longed to go to the station to meet Kurt. I begged to be able to leave the house just for once. But my friends gently but firmly prevented me. I put on my best clothes. I waited in a fever of expectation.

At last he arrived. And I had a shock. This man

was not the blithe, gay youth I had been so much in love with. I was stunned. He had lines of a man of fifty on his face. His hair was nearly white. And the grand physique I had admired had vanished. The shoulders were bowed, the chest sunken.

I tried to overlook it all because he was so obviously happy to see me. I kissed him, I laughed, I cried. I tried to pretend I had noticed hardly any change. But it was no use. Kurt himself was only too well aware of it.

He laughed bitterly : "You see what political education at a concentration-camp has done for me, Pauline. I am now supposed to be fit to become a citizen of the Reich."

Poor Kurt. He had been treated terribly badly. He told me a tale of beating, hard labour, short rations of bad food which was only too familiar to me. It was the same story that hundreds of thousands of others could tell.

We had a little party that night. There was good food, good wine, and good music—all provided by our friends. They were glad to have the excuse for a little gaiety for once, I think, for their days were rarely anything but tragic for somebody.

And now the end of my story approaches. We were wondering how to get to France or England when the chief of the organization which was sheltering us discovered in conversation with Kurt that his birth at Haguenau, which is in Alsace-Lorraine entitled him to choose French citizenship if he wished.

You cannot imagine as dwellers in a free land what this tremendous discovery meant to us. It was as though we were doomed to hell, and found the gates of heaven opening for us instead.

We went to the French Consul-General, and found that sympathetic man ready to complete the formalities of citizenship for both of us at top speed.

And so we came to France, not as refugees, as we had dared to hope, but as citizens of the freest republic in the world, to the home of liberty.

I am writing these last few lines in a little flat on the third floor of a building in Montmartre.

Kurt has been called up for military service in the French Army. Gladly he went. I have a job at my old trade of laundering. My pay is less than half the wages Hitler paid me. It seems riches in this land where even the air smells of freedom. Sometimes at night I dream of Dachau and Berchtesgaden. I see the mutilated face of poor Otto Schlieben, the leering eyes of Hausmann. I hear the grating voice of Adolf Hitler himself. I find myself awaiting sentence from the Secret Police.

I said I dreamed. . . .

I was wrong. These are nightmares in France.

THE END